PATTERNS FOR
LIFE'S PILGRIMS

Patterns for Life's Pilgrims

R. L. Middleton

BROADMAN PRESS · NASHVILLE, TENNESSEE

© Copyright 1967 · BROADMAN PRESS
NASHVILLE, TENNESSEE
All rights reserved
422–334

DEWEY DECIMAL CLASSIFICATION NUMBER: 68–12562
LIBRARY OF CONGRESS CATALOG CARD NUMBER: 248.4
Printed in the United States of America
5.O67KSP

Foreword

They were a courageous group of 102 people who set sail from Southampton, England, September 16, 1620, seeking a land where they might worship without interference from the Church of England. They spoke of themselves as "pilgrims" because they had set out on a pilgrimage in search of religious freedom. For some twenty years they had moved from place to place in their home country and become known as Separatists because they had separated from the State Church.

Approximately sixty days later they sighted land and moved into Providencetown Harbor, at the tip of Cape Cod, Massachusetts. They named their little colony Plymouth in memory of the town of Plymouth, England.

The first year at Plymouth these brave souls were clinging frantically to the small thread of life. During the winter, forty-seven of the group were buried in the frozen soil. Nevertheless they had ventured forth on faith, and despite their hardships were grateful to God for his blessings. They were mostly persons of humble birth and occupation, but deep in their hearts there was a love for God. With a desire to express their thanks they set aside a special day to acknowledge the good things which had happened to them. From this experience we have our Thanksgiving Day. Many are the "patterns" worthy of emulation which this noble group left as a heritage for their sacrifices for religious freedom.

As much as we would honor these men and women of the Plymouth Colony, it is my hope and purpose in these messages to stress the fact that life is a pilgrimage and we are pilgrims. We need help, guidelines, "patterns" along the journey. As the children of Israel journeyed on their pilgrimage toward the Promised Land, God spoke to Jacob in a dream as he slept on the stones at Bethel, saying: "Behold, I am with thee, and will keep thee in all places whither thou goest, and will bring thee again into this land; for I will not leave thee, until I have done that which I have spoken to thee of" (Gen. 28:15).

God has promised to be the guide for his pilgrims as they journey through this world, and his promises still hold true if we will follow his leadership, his patterns along the way.

Jesus calls us o'er the tumult
  Of our life's wild, restless sea;
Day by day His sweet voice soundeth,
  Saying, "Christian, *follow me!*"

Jesus calls us from the worship
  Of the vain world's golden store,
From each idol that would keep us,
  Saying, "Christian, *love me more.*"

In our joys and in our sorrows,
  Days of toil and hours of ease,
Still He calls, in cares and pleasures,
  "Christian, *love me more than these.*"

> Jesus calls us: by Thy mercies,
>   Saviour, may we hear Thy call,
> Give our hearts to Thine obedience,
>   *Serve and love Thee best of all.*

Fellow pilgrims, may we answer his call; may we seek his patterns for life's journey!

R. L. MIDDLETON

In all good things shewing thyself a *pattern* of good works: in doctrine shewing uncorruptness, gravity, sincerity, sound speech, that cannot be condemned; that he that is of the contrary part may be ashamed, having no evil thing to say of you (*Titus 2:7–8*).

Contents

1
Patterns for Pilgrims

Life is a pilgrimage and we the pilgrims along the highway. The journey oftentimes is hard and we need patterns along the way.

Our Saviour was a pilgrim, and even before his earthly ministry was begun he was led by the Spirit into the wilderness to be tempted—tempted just as we will be along life's journey. He did not find all the answers at once. Only after much trouble of soul, searching in prayer, and care in thought did our Lord find the solutions he sought. Through these experiences Jesus identified himself with each of us. The Galilean found the answers, leaving trail marks, guidelines, patterns for our decisions. Some of them we hope to discover in these messages.

Over two hundred years ago, two brothers, Peter and William Williams, sensed the need for guidance for all Christians when they wrote the beloved hymn "Guide Me, O Thou Great Jehovah":

> Guide, me, O thou great Jehovah,
>   Pilgrim through this barren land;
> I am weak, but thou art mighty;
>   Hold me with thy powerful hand.

Open now the crystal fountains
  Whence the living waters flow;
Let the fiery, cloudy pillar
  Lead me all my journey through.

Feed me with the heavenly manna
  In this barren wilderness;
Be my sword, and shield, and banner,
  Be the Lord my Righteousness.

When I tread the verge of Jordan,
  Bid my anxious fears subside;
Death of death, and hell's destruction,
  Land me safe on Canaan's side.

The word "pattern" is a simple word, yet when its full meaning and usage are studied it proves to be most fascinating. At first glance, one is not aware of its many implications, of how one's life is guided or misguided by the patterns he follows. We dress by a pattern, comb our hair by a pattern, choose our clothes according to the styles (patterns) set by manufacturers. It's an old saying that we are creatures of habit and it's true; but patterns bring on these habits.

Look quickly at a few definitions given in the dictionary: A pattern is "that after which something is made, something which is worthy of imitation; a model, an ideal, an example, a specimen. A mold into which molten metal is poured to form a casting; a specimen of a proposed coin, minted before its authorization as currency." There are others, but to put it simply, a pattern is "something to be copied."

In France in the Imperial Library, one of the oldest libraries in the world, is a copybook of Louis XIV in which the young despot wrote six times on one page, "Homage belongs to kings: they do whatsoever it pleases them to do."

Copybooks have apparently disappeared from our grammar school curricula. I never hear of them any more, but how well I remember the copybook for handwriting I used as a boy. Over and over again we would copy the sentence at the top of the page, using a system of freehand penmanship devised by Herbert Spencer about 1855. Schoolchildren would profit by such a copybook today.

In few areas of life is there a more urgent need for patterns to be set than in our homes of today. The pattern or copy that the family and society in general sets for children is far-reaching in its effect. The whole question of early training—do we not see with what fine tools it must do its work in order that the child may learn values?

The family is the most important school in which the human being carries on his studies. Every hour the child is a learner, following his copy. If the copy is worldly, the lesson sinks unconsciously into his soul; and he in turn is likely to become a little worldling. Parental conversation in the den or family room or at the table will often set the child's habits like cement. Talk of worldly things is infectious: the father returning in the evening with his increasing talk of world values and never a hint of life's higher values; the mother returning to her nest with no message for the children except empty echoes of card parties and theater parties and new clothes. What sad copies are these to set before youthful minds!

But there are parents who cherish the privilege which is theirs in guiding children in the ways of righteousness, of love and loyalty toward one another; and these lessons will go with the children through life.

There is a touching story that was attributed to Dr. Leslie Weatherhead when he was minister of City Temple in London. He described how a small boy, a waif, was brought into a home for children. The matron who met this little boy said to him, "Now there's one thing we have to do. We've got to ask you for the clothes you have on, and we're going to give you a nice warm bath, and then you will get some new clothes." The little boy obeyed but held onto his cap. He tore out the lining and put it in his pocket. The matron asked, "Why did you do that?" And he replied, "Ma'am, that lining was made from my mother's dress, and it's the only thing I have left now that brings her close to me. Let me keep it." Somewhere back in the past that mother had endeared herself to the lad in such a way that he could never forget. He was just a little pilgrim along life's way, but he had witnessed patterns of love and devotion, perhaps even sacrifices, which would abide forever. May God give us more mothers whose influence will be a monument to them as their children grow into men and women.

I can remember in my boyhood days seeing my mother, or a neighbor seamstress, laying a piece of cloth on the dining room table, placing a "tissue pattern" on top of it, pinning it in place, then cutting the material from which some article of clothing would be made for one of her children. Such a process has been followed for hundreds of years.

Now, modern machinery and manufacturing plants have just about eliminated "homemade" clothes. However, if you go to one of these large manufacturing plants, there on the cutting table will be the cloth—forty or fifty or more thicknesses—which will be cut by modern machinery. A pattern has been previously built into the machine. This is basic for the design of the garment being planned.

A newspaper headline in July, 1966, reported the death of Sy Devore of Hollywood, California. His customers, people of prominence and wealth, ranged from President Johnson to such well-known movie and TV celebrities as Milton Berle, Jerry Lewis, John Wayne, and Sammy Davis, Jr. His custom-made suits ranged in price from $300 to $450. Lewis was reported as a $75,000-a-year customer. Bob Hope once commented: "In a very good year I had my choice between a Rolls-Royce, a new home in Beverly Hills, or a suit from Sy Devore." Back of all of these expensive clothes there had to be the special cloth, a special design perhaps; but always the pattern was basic.

The use of patterns goes far beyond the clothing industry. It is followed in every phase of manufacturing. In shoe manufacturing plants every part of the finished product must first be cut from leather, according to pattern. In gas and electric stove plants a large sheet of flat steel is placed on a giant press, and down comes the mold (pattern) under great pressure. Then, out comes a perfectly formed stove door, or some other integral part.

At General Motors, there are four major steps carried out over a three-year period. Each new model does not get its start in steel, glass, rubber, and plastic. Each car begins in the designer's mind, takes tentative shape on a scratch pad, then a more permanent form on a drawing board.

Once the preliminary drawing, blown up to a full-scale model, is approved, the next step is a clay model, showing roof lines and front and rear ends, all of which must be balanced in the integrated body shape. This clay model is painted and chromed with aluminum foil to give it as realistic a look as possible. The actual dimensions and surface drawings are taken directly from this clay model pattern. The final step, however, is the fiber-glass model, finished on the exterior and interior in detail. From this the steel molds are cast, the various parts produced.

The modern automobile contains more than four thousand parts—steel, rubber, plastic, upholstery, the electric system, and so on—and for every item there must be a pattern.

In the field of athletics, whether it be high school, college, or professional teams and baseball, football, or basketball, there is a basic pattern for every play. Watch the pattern when the quarterback calls for a pass to an end or a halfback. The intended receiver will go straight down the field ten yards, cut to his left a few paces, then turn sharply toward the sidelines where the pass is to be thrown. All of these fakes and movements are designed to outwit the defense. If the pattern is followed correctly, the pass may be successful. The success of a winning team often depends on whether the play patterns are known and carried out.

Turn to an entirely different area of life, that of our National Government. They were brave and dedicated men who patterned our Constitution and Declaration of Independence. These documents and their meaning should be precious in the hearts and minds of every American—in fact, of all the world. Likewise, the United Nations organization and its charter were patterned in such a way as to hope for world peace. May God speed the day.

There are few days as significant in the life of a prospective bride as the one on which she selects the pattern for her silver and china, crystal, and other items which she hopes to cherish always. God gave the pattern for marriage in Mark 10:9: "What therefore God hath joined together, let not man put asunder." A home can never be a happy one unless God's patterns are followed.

As we attend the worship services of our churches on Sunday, an usher gives us a bulletin, or an order of service. It is a "pattern" to be followed as God draws nigh to us and we draw nigh to him through the singing of hymns, prayers, giving of our tithes and offerings, and the sermon from God's minister.

Patterns will often determine our destiny, our well-being,

our happiness, our success, or our disappointments. Life is so precious, and each of us has an eternal destiny.

When asked the secret of his radiant and successful life, General Booth—founder of the Salvation Army—replied, "Jesus has had all of me." One has only to read his life to discover that he wholeheartedly and unreservedly followed the teachings of Christ every step of the way.

We make demands of life, and just as surely as we do, life makes its demands on us. Our Saviour does so many things for us when we face life's demands. "The Son of man is not come to destroy men's lives, but to save them" (Luke 9:56). Yes, he came to show us the way of salvation and eternal life.

It is my hope and prayer that through these messages we, as pilgrims, may discover anew some of the patterns needed for life's journey, and I know of no better guidebook than God's Guidebook.

> Holy Bible, Book divine,
> Precious treasure, thou art mine.
> Mine to tell me whence I came;
> Mine to teach me what I am.
>
> Mine to chide me when I rove,
> Mine to show a Saviour's love;
> Mine thou art to guide my feet,
> Mine to judge, condemn, acquit.
>
> Mine to comfort in distress,
> If the Holy Spirit bless;
> Mine to show by living faith
> Man can triumph over death.
>
> Mine to tell of joys to come,
> And the rebel sinner's doom;
> Holy Bible, Book divine,
> Precious treasure, thou art mine.

2
Old Testament Patterns

One of Nashville's most popular radio-TV stations, WSM, has been made famous for its Grand Ole Opry programs, heard all across the country. Another one of its award-winning programs is "The Noon Show," on which prominent local and visiting personalities are featured. It is well diversified, but always there is a guest minister for about a ten-minute interview. A few years ago Dr. Frank F. Drowota, minister of the Woodmont Christian Church, was asked by the announcer, "We would like to discuss the Bible this week. Will you give us a layman's definition of the Bible?" Without hesitation, he answered, *"The Bible is a Book in which God has a word for you and for me."* He then gave numerous examples of Scripture verses he frequently recommended, especially to new church members. Dr. Drowota could as easily have said, "The Bible is a Book in which God suggests *patterns for life's pilgrims*—patterns for Christian living—lessons from heaven for life on earth."

The Bible is more than a book. It is the living Word of God, breathed from eternity into time for redemption, enlightenment, welfare, and guidance of men. It is the voice of God, speaking to the heart of humanity through the ages. It stands alone in human literature in its elevated conception of manhood, in character and conduct. The books of men have their day and grow obsolete. God's Word is like himself, "the same yesterday, today, and forever."

Because God breathed himself into the words that make up the Bible, they are one with him, dynamic, eternal, and supreme. In these troubled times we need to rethink the patterns of our lives, to catch a new vision of what God can do for us through a study of his holy Word.

The *law* of the Lord is perfect, converting the soul: the *testimony* of the Lord is sure, making wise the simple. The *statutes* of the Lord are right, rejoicing the heart: the *commandment* of the Lord is pure, enlightening the eyes. The *fear* of the Lord is clean, enduring for ever: the *judgments* of the Lord are true and righteous altogether. More to be desired are they than gold, yea, than much fine gold: sweeter also than honey and the honeycomb (Psalm 19:7–10).

The creation.—Read again the first chapter of Genesis and observe the minute pattern God followed in the creation of the world, climaxing it with the creation of man in his own image. Then watch the pattern further as you read the second chapter. "On the seventh day God ended his work which he had made; and he rested on the seventh day from all his work which he had made. And God blessed the seventh day, and sanctified it: because that in it he had rested from all his work which God created and made" (vv. 2–3). Thus, as early as the creation of the world, God planned a day of rest and worship for his children. But how far the world has strayed from this pattern!

We are living in what has become known as the "space age." To my mind, all of these fantastic efforts to reach the moon are useless dreams. What if we do, what have we gained? God set the moon, the sun, and the stars in an orderly pattern and they will remain in that pattern throughout eternity.

The sun, the source of all of our life, is said to have a surface temperature of 12,000° Fahrenheit, and our earth is far enough away so that this "eternal fire" warms us just enough and not too much. If the sun gave off only one half of its present radiation, we would freeze; and if it gave this much more we would almost roast. God just planned it that way.

The earth rotates on its axis one thousand miles an hour; if it turned at one hundred miles an hour, our days and nights would be ten times as long as now. The hot sun would burn up our vegetation each day while in the long night any surviving sprout would freeze.

No human being can alter the design of the hundreds of different leaves on a designated tree, nor the colors of the flowers, nor the plumage and songs of God's songbirds. These are all patterned by the Master Artist.

Again, God created the fish of the sea, and gave them a pattern of living. The young salmon spends years at sea, then comes back to his own river, and travels up the very side of the river into which flows the tributary where he was born. What brings him back so precisely? Instinct, yes! But who gave him that instinct—that pattern for life? Nature did not create life in these animals. Only God did.

But let's come closer to home.

The Ten Commandments.—One of the oldest patterns for daily living is the Ten Commandments, given to Moses approximately 3,500 years ago. All through the Scriptures they are referred to as the Law. Did not Jesus himself say, "I am not come to destroy [the law], but to fulfil [it]" (Matt. 5:17)? Read the Commandments again in Exodus 20 and note carefully how each one of these simple but positive statements can be applied to our daily lives. Look at the roll call of sins which would be eliminated, making for a better world and a happier place in which to live, if these patterns were followed.

The "pure gold" of these Commandments clearly reflected the nature and purpose of God; yet the children of Israel, in an effort to give their own interpretation to them, wove many tapestries of tradition over their brightness and their purpose. Eventually, traditions which they themselves had created were all they could see. Their full meaning as patterns for daily living had become entirely shrouded, and they had lost much of what God had set forth as guidelines for Christian living. Are we, like the children of Israel, letting the cares of today's fast pace of living pull us away from these sacred precepts, these God-given guides to a happier life?

The Psalms.—Page after page of the Old Testament is filled with golden nuggets, rich in God's design and purpose for a better way of life. Few things in all literature can compare with the beauty and warmth of the psalms of David. Here is recorded the genuineness of a heart eternally grateful to a loving God. Here we find a soul which had wandered into the paths of sin and unrighteousness but which found its way back to God (see Psalm 51).

Two of my favorites of these precious gems are Psalms 1 and 103. A practice of our pastor, Dr. H. Franklin Paschall, is to have a brief conference with each candidate for baptism just prior to the evening service. A five-minute devotion is a part of this conference, and it was my privilege to lead this devotional for about a year. I first read twelve verses from Psalm 103, stressing all the blessings God has given every Christian. Then I followed this reading with the beautiful picture or pattern of the godly man as described by David. I invite you to read it carefully, slowly, and meditate upon it. Note the pattern as it unfolds: "Blessed is the man that *walketh not* in the counsel of the ungodly, *nor standeth* in the way of sinners, *nor sitteth* in the seat of the scornful. But *his delight* is in the law of the Lord; and *in his law doth he meditate day and night*" (1:1–2, author's italics).

Now note the reward of the ungodly man who does not follow God's pattern: "The ungodly are not so: but are like the chaff which the wind driveth away. Therefore the ungodly shall not stand in the judgment, nor sinners in the congregation of the righteous. For the Lord knoweth the way of the righteous: but the way of the ungodly shall perish" (vv. 4–6).

All through the Psalms David so many times expresses his gratitude to God and utters words of praise and thanksgiving. He learned his lessons the hard way because in a weak moment he departed from God's pattern for a happy and rewarding life.

Isaiah's vision.—Look quickly at the transforming vision which came to Isaiah as recorded in the sixth chapter. King Uzziah had died. In his sorrow and despondency, Isaiah went to the Temple, seeking guidance and consolation. He saw the Lord sitting upon a throne, high and lifted up. He saw him in a new light, and in a heart searching for solace and comfort, he cried: "Woe is me! for I am undone; because I am a man of unclean lips, and I dwell in the midst of a people of unclean lips: for mine eyes have seen the King, the Lord of hosts. . . . Also I heard the voice of the Lord, saying, Whom shall I send, and who will go for us? Then said I, Here am I; send me" (Isa. 6:5–8).

God answered, "Go, and tell this people." Through this moving encounter with God, Isaiah had found his answer to a hungry heart, a new pattern for life's days. *God had a word for Isaiah.*

Solomon's advice in Proverbs.—This collection of pithy sayings is just as applicable today in its divine wisdom as it was in Solomon's time. The first seven chapters of Proverbs are devoted almost exclusively to advice for young men, and would be equally appropriate for young women. One brief quotation is typical, and so often quoted:

My son, forget not my law; but let thine heart keep my commandments: For length of days, and long life, and peace, shall they add to thee. Let not mercy and truth forsake thee: bind them about thy neck; write them upon the table of thine heart: so shalt thou find favour and good understanding in the sight of God and man. Trust in the Lord with all thine heart; and lean not unto thine own understanding. In all thy ways acknowledge him, and he shall direct thy paths (3:1-6).

Space will not permit a roll call of God's prophets and other godly men of Old Testament history, but you may read for yourself the long list of heroes as recorded in the eleventh chapter of Hebrews. These stalwart souls clung to the patterns God gave as guidelines for a happier way of life.

In this Divine Library—written in different lands, among different races, in widely different ages, by widely different men—these books gathered themselves together from their various sources and became, in the course of human life, welded together into a unity. The secret of this unity is that it all centers in Jesus Christ. The Bible is always a picture of Christ, a beautiful portrait in an appropriate frame. The reason the world needs the Bible, needs to search the Scriptures, is because the world needs Christ, and the world cannot find Christ sufficiently except in the Bible.

It is a Book not to be worshiped but to be studied. Here

we will find the unanswerable proof of the experiences of individuals in the life and communities of their day. God found the Israelites in Egypt of old. The first thing he did was to redeem them, and to give them a better way of life. God saw the world as it was nineteen hundred years ago, and what he did was to send his only begotten Son to redeem the world of lost men. The Bible is the record, not only in the Old Testament but also and perhaps even more clearly in the New Testament, of a clear and ever-growing revelation of God as a faithful and unchangeable Redeemer of men. Let us look, then, in the New Testament for even more striking examples of God's patterns for Christian living.

3
New Testament Patterns

We have observed in the previous chapter how God in his infinite wisdom, from the very beginning of creation, planned a way of Christian living for his children. He never gave up hope, climaxing his plans and program with the coming of his Son. Through Christ and his example, his precepts, his teachings, we have patterns for Christian living the like of which no human could have conceived.

Christ was not only the master teacher but also the master preacher, always pouring out his great heart, seeking men to follow his way of life. Perhaps the greatest example of his preaching is the unmatched Sermon on the Mount. Near the close of this message, as recorded in Luke 6, our Lord seems to have become impatient with his listeners. He knew that many of the people gathered before him on the side of the mountain appeared to be interested, but they would go away and quickly forget everything he had said. Attempting to drive home his demand for wholehearted loyalty on the part of those who would follow him, he asked, "Why call ye me Lord, Lord, and do not the things which I say?" (Luke 6:46). He followed up this question with the story of a man who built his house on a rock, and it stood. And then of a

second man who built a house on the sands, and it fell. Why?
Both men had called Christ "Lord! Lord!" but one had not
heeded his patterns for success in daily living. Jesus de-
manded wholehearted loyalty of all his disciples.

Throughout the Gospels and the writings of Paul, there
are teachings which our world desperately needs—teachings
and admonitions which should, and would, transform every
follower of Christ. Olin T. Binkley, in a sermon "A Charter
for Christian Living," drives home the necessity for a change
in attitude in churches and individuals.

The climate of thought in American society is changing. There
is a resurgence of interest in the spiritual foundations of life, and
people are turning to the churches for moral guidance. . . .
Church members are thinking seriously about the vital issues in
our divided and frightened world, and they are asking penetrating
questions. What is the ideal of personal character? What are the
moral principles of Christian action? How does Jesus Christ
desire his disciples to think, speak, and act in our complex and
changing social order? How can we translate faith into deed?

This quest for moral insight and courage draws us to a fresh
study of the Bible. When we read the New Testament with
teachable minds and tender hearts, we hear the call of the
Master to seek first the kingdom of God and his righteousness.
We learn how to examine human problems in the perspective of
the sovereignty of God. We discover that the direction of Christian action in concrete situations is to be determined by reference to what God has done for us in Christ. We receive stimulus
to develop a mature sense of moral responsibility, to order our
lives by the ethic of justice and love which our Lord set out to
establish on earth, and to participate in the adventure of Christian living in a revolutionary age.[1]

---

[1] *Christian Faith in Action,* comp. Foy Valentine (Nashville: Broadman Press, 1956), pp. 126–27.

In all of the teachings of Jesus, there are patterns for Christian living which could only have been conceived in the heart of our Saviour.

Jesus and the Samaritan woman.—This is a familiar story, but we may ask, "Why did Jesus choose to go through Samaria when he and his disciples knew of the unfriendliness of the Jews for the Samaritans?" He went seeking to fill a need which he knew existed, seeking to touch human hearts. He did not know in advance of the woman at the well, but he did know that there were many individuals who needed a new pattern for Christian living.

Beginning with a conversation about water, Jesus was quick to probe her past. The kind of life she had lived had left its mark—depraved, despised, disgraced in the eyes of her friends. No doubt she had secretly asked the question, "Is life worth living? Are all the days to be like those of recent years?" In every person there is this unsatisfied longing, this vague discontent, this emptiness, this something lacking, this longing for that which gives a meaningful existence. The dissatisfied, restless soul is never without this inward quest.

Even though the question of where one should worship had entered the conversation, Jesus was quick to detect a soul seeking to find meaning to life. Deep in the heart of this sinful woman there was this hunger, despite the wretched life she had been living. In Christ she found "living water" to quench her soul's thirst. In him and his way of righteousness, she found life with meaning, a new pattern for the days ahead. Overjoyed, she hastened back into the city, and said to the men, "Come, see a man, which told me all things that ever I did: is not this the Christ? Then they went out of the city and came unto him" (John 4:29–30). A lost soul had found a Saviour.

Jesus and Nicodemus.—The story of the coming of Nicodemus to Jesus is another one of those fascinating incidents
described by John. The scene is set in Jerusalem. It is evening. Dusk has fallen, and through the shadowy streets we
see a hooded figure on a journey, seeking an interview with
the young prophet of Nazareth. It is done under cover of
darkness, but this is no itinerant traveler seeking a meeting
with Jesus. It is Nicodemus, one of the leaders of the Jews
and a member of the Sanhedrin. Like every devout Jew,
Nicodemus was concerned with the coming of the kingdom
of God, but like so many others he had confused it in his
thinking with the idea of politics, power, and prestige.

Note the respect with which he greets Jesus: "Rabbi, we
know that thou art a teacher come from God: for no man can
do these miracles that thou doest, except God be with him"
(John 3:2). Jesus then sets forth the pattern of the new
birth, without which one cannot see the kingdom of God. He
immediately points his visitor to the true fact that the kingdom which he is proclaiming can only be entered when one
has been reborn or realizes anew the spiritual presence of
God in his life. Rebirth will not come about from beneath; it
will come from above. It does not come from the flesh, but
from the spirit. Without a change in the inner man one is
never a true follower of Christ.

All of the details of the interview are probably not in-
cluded in the Gospel narrative. How long they were together
we cannot say, but out of this meeting has come the very
foundation of Christianity—regeneration, a new birth, a new
nature, a new set of desires, a new way to look at things,
even a new will. We can imagine Jesus saying to his visitor,
"It isn't something we can do for ourselves, Nicodemus. Only
God can work this miracle."

Few of us understand the actual regeneration which takes

place in the lives of individuals, but we have seen it take place. And thanks to Nicodemus, we have this cardinal truth set forth.

The interview ended, perhaps late in the night. He looked into Christ's eyes, gripped his hands, departed, and retraced his steps homeward. What was in the mind and heart of Nicodemus as he recalled the pattern set forth by our Saviour? Did he become a secret disciple?

The weeks and months pass, and Nicodemus is not heard from again until cruel plans are being made for our Saviour's death. Jesus has been seized by the soldiers in the garden of Gethsemane and hailed before Annas, who sends him bound unto Caiphas, the high priest. The Feast of the Tabernacles is in its last day when the seventy-one members of the Sanhedrin are solemnly assembled in the Temple to hear the charges against an innocent man. Never has there been such mockery. Through all of the bickering back and forth, what is going through the heart and thoughts of Nicodemus? I believe we can justly assume that he was pricked to the core as he witnessed this miscarriage of justice.

Why do I venture such an assumption?

After the crucifixion is over, John tells us:

After this Joseph of Arimathaea, being a disciple of Jesus, but secretly for fear of the Jews, besought Pilate that he might take away the body of Jesus: and Pilate gave him leave. He came therefore, and took the body of Jesus. *And there came also Nicodemus,* which at the first came to Jesus by night, and brought a mixture of myrrh and aloes, about an hundred pound weight. Then took they the body of Jesus, and wound it in linen clothes with the spices, as the manner of the Jews is to bury (19:38–40).

There are some terrible scenes in the Gospel accounts of the life of Christ, but the crucifixion was the most cruel. Had

Nicodemus been a secret disciple? Had he been following Christ's cardinal pattern of regeneration, the new birth? We would like to hope this was true, but oh! the tragedy of a life which could have meant so much to the coming of the kingdom of God, if he had only been a daily witness for Christ.

Jesus and Zacchaeus.—Jesus was passing through Jericho, the home of a wealthy man named Zacchaeus. Why did this man seek to learn more about our Saviour? He had probably seen and heard of the transformation in people's lives, of the miracles being performed. His very effort to come in contact with Christ is evidence of a hunger for something which was lacking in his life.

In one of his sermons, Lloyd C. Douglas, the masterful religious novelist, has described this meeting of Jesus and Zacchaeus in a most dramatic way. This description is printed below:

Sitting across the dinner table from the Galilean, Zacchaeus is pictured as bragging of his authority, his possessions, and his self-importance. Through it all the Master sits silently. His eyes pierced with conviction the heart of the foolish man's life. Finally Zacchaeus went to the porch and told the waiting mob that he was willing to pay back, restore, and give away; for at last he had found that "things" did not matter. When he returned to the table, Jesus said, "Zacchaeus, what did you see that made you desire this peace?" Came the reply, "Good Master, I saw mirrored in your eyes, the face of the Zacchaeus I was meant to be."

Such a gaze, such an experience can redeem us from the meaninglessness and lostness we have known. Before we set out upon the experiences of each new day, we can afford to take a fresh look at our own lives.[2]

----

[2] As quoted by Wyburn Skidmore, *The Upper Room,* January–February, 1951, p. 25.

These three illustrations from the Gospels cannot begin to give us the joy which can be ours if we will only pursue a further study of the storehouse of guidelines for daily living as Christians. As Dr. Binkley so beautifully stated: "When we read the New Testament with teachable minds and tender hearts, we hear the call of the Master to seek first the kingdom of God and his righteousness. We learn how to examine human problems in the perspective of the sovereignty of God."

Let us search the Scriptures as we continue life's pilgrimage. Like a lighthouse for ships at sea, loaded with passengers and travel-worn workmen, the Gospels and the writings of Paul are challenging and rewarding studies. "Thy word is a lamp unto my feet, and a light unto my path" (Psalm 119:105).

4
Keys to Abundant Living

For hundreds and hundreds of years it has been the historic practice of city and state officials to present to visiting dignitaries a key to the city or state. The key is considered a symbol of public trust and faith in the recipient and a welcome to the community.

Keys are older than history itself. Even in the earliest days of the Egyptians, keys had their symbolic meanings. Keys in biblical times were a badge of office and were carried over the right shoulder. One illustration is the type of key referred to by the prophet Isaiah in the Scriptures: "The key of the house of David will I lay upon his shoulder; so he shall open, and none shall shut; and he shall shut, and none shall open" (22:22). A key was, and is, a badge of power and authority. In the first mention of the church Jesus said to Peter, "I will give unto thee the keys of the kingdom of heaven: and whatsoever thou shalt bind on earth shall be bound in heaven: and whatsoever thou shalt loose on earth shall be loosed in heaven" (Matt. 16:19).

Apostolic history explains and limits this trust, for it was Peter who opened the door of Christian opportunity to Israel on the day of Pentecost (Acts 2:38–42), and to Gentiles in the house of Cornelius (10:34–46). He came to see that God is no respecter of persons.

Because keys have meant security and protection, locksmiths of old were pledged to "fidelity and secrecy" and were considered custodians of public safety. Few craftsmen achieved this respected position in their community. When they did, they were required to display in their shops the symbol of membership in the craftsman's guild. Many of the more famous makers of keys followed the trade as a family tradition for hundreds of years.

Through the years, keys have reflected not only the artistic standards of their periods but also the historical events. One of the most famous keys is the one to the notorious prison in Paris, the Bastille. After France showed a more humanitarian attitude toward its prisoners, and after the closing of the Bastille, this key was presented by the French to George Washington in August, 1790, as a symbol of the new freedom of the Republic of France. It may be seen today in Washington's historic home, Mount Vernon.

Every Christian must possess spiritual keys if he is to live an abundant life. The keynote of Christianity is *love*. It was God's love for a lost humanity that caused him to send his Son into the world that the world might be saved. And Jesus, recognizing the power of love, over and over again voiced its need in the life of every Christian. In a discussion with the scribes and Sadducees he was interrupted by one, a lawyer, asking, "Which is the first commandment of all?"

Jesus answered him, The first of all the commandments is, Hear, O Israel; the Lord our God is one Lord: and thou shalt love the Lord thy God with all thy heart, and with all thy soul, and with all thy mind, and with all thy strength: this is the first commandment. And the second is like, namely this, Thou shalt love thy neighbor as thyself. There is none other commandment greater than these (Mark 12:29–31).

Perhaps no other word in our language is so often misused, so frequently misapplied as the word love. Movies, television, radio, and stage plays have downgraded the real meaning of love until it has lost much of its impact. Yet the definitions of this term, even by the latest dictionaries, leave one cold. One who really knows the meaning of love (and he can learn it from life's experience alone) feels that a mere definition is inadequate for a word that can have a significance so deep and splendid. Its meaning is too complex, its nature too venerable to be comprehended in a mere definition. Love moves in an orbit far greater than any yet discovered by an astronomer. The dictionary gives us direction as to how we may, in a small way, understand the magnitude of this almost holy virtue.

Love means ardent affection; it means superior regard; it means solicitude for the welfare of another. Love is seldom found in the marketplace. It is never found associated with personal ambition or with selfishness, jealousy, or greed. Perhaps the Bible can give us the best definition, the best pattern, the best example of genuine love: "God so *loved* . . . that he *gave*."

Completely understood, that statement carries one great revelation about love: it walks side by side, hand in hand with selfless generosity. Love can never be demonstrated unless it is willing to sacrifice for the recipient. That is what God did. That is what Paul was trying to say in his magnificent "Ode to Love" as found in 1 Corinthians 13. We will not quote it all because it is one of the most loved, the most quoted by ministers, the crowning appraisal of one who had known life in all its ways, and one who had come to lead an abundant life of service through devotion to Christ our Saviour. (The word "love" has been substituted for "charity.")

Love suffereth long, and is kind; love envieth not; love vaunteth not itself, is not puffed up, doth not behave itself unseemly, seeketh not her own, is not easily provoked, thinketh no evil; rejoiceth not in iniquity, but rejoiceth in the truth; beareth all things, believeth all things, hopeth all things, endureth all things. Love never faileth: but whether there be prophecies, they shall fail; whether there be tongues, they shall cease; whether there be knowledge, it shall vanish away. . . . And now abideth faith, hope, love, these three; but the greatest of these is love (vv. 4–13).

Henry Drummond has pictured these abiding graces of love as a spectrum with nine ingredients. Note how beautiful they are: patience, kindness, generosity, humility, courtesy, unselfishness, good temper, guilelessness, and sincerity. All of these are keys to an abundant life—patterns for Christian living.

Genuine love requires *action*. Christ knew this. Was he not forever urging people to act? "This *do* in remembrance of me." "Go, and *do* likewise." "If ye love me *keep* my commandments." In short, if you care for me, prove your affection by your behavior. If faith without works is vain, love without action is vain also. Love is too vital a principle to be realized by mere thinking, dreaming, and well-wishing.

The whole story of the relationship of love in action was never more classically illustrated than in the story of the good Samaritan as told by Jesus. No doubt the priest and the Levite felt sorry for the wounded wayfarer, but not sorry enough. They refused actively to help. Every situation in which trouble is involved is love's opportunity. Depend upon it; love never passes by on the other side.

Look again at just three of the ingredients of Drummond's spectrum of love: patience, kindness, unselfishness. Into the home of two of our dearest friends, a husband and wife several years our senior, tragedy came with the birth of their fourth daughter. The first three children were perfect babies and were to grow into beautiful young women, marry well, and have extremely happy homes. But the last daughter was a spastic and retarded from birth, a lovable personality, yet marred by the crippling aspects of the misfortune with which she was born. For nearly forty years now the devoted mother and father have never left her unattended a minute. Patience, kindness, sympathy, understanding, unselfishness, courtesy, and every evidence possible of human compassion have attended the child, to whom we are devoted. *Love in action* has been the God-given attribute and grace of these noble parents.

Love is the spirit of God in the human heart; and to have this abiding love, demonstrated so beautifully by these parents, is merely to ally oneself with him—to perform with him and for him the mission he has for us in bringing about his kingdom on earth. Love never fails, and in this life of so many earthly things passing away, we long for things that endure. Love is a spiritual virtue available to all. "A Song of Love," written by an unknown poet, speaks of its value.

> Guard it ever faithful,
> Hold it ever fast;
> 'Tis the only treasure
> That will ever last.
>
> Be your heart its garden,
> Your care its sun and shade;
> 'Tis the only flower
> That will never fade.

Keep its rapture singing;
Let all else go by;
'Tis the only music
That will never die.

Follow it, though rugged
Be the path and strange;
'Tis the only beauty
That will never change.

Follow, follow after,
Over land and foam;
'Tis the only comrade
That will lead you home.

A second key to abundant living is that of service and sacrifice. If our Christianity is to have reality, it must bear fruit in action. We have already said that love must be active if it stems from a heart dedicated to Christ. Our lives must find expression in service, whether in small services to those with whom we come in contact daily or in services to greater causes which are instruments of God's will. The spiritual foundation of Christianity is the law of sacrifice, the gift of oneself in some worthy cause. Nor must our gifts be confined to the things of the body. They should be the gifts of the whole man—spirit, soul, and body. *"He that loseth his life shall find it"* is not merely a pious saying. It is a sentence endowed with profound significance; a truth, a pattern exemplified by our Saviour. It is a law of the heart of Christianity.

Never have I been so challenged by an example of unselfish, sacrificial service as by a story told by Cecil Sherman, pastor of the First Baptist Church, Asheville, North Carolina. Don Burgess, age twenty-six, works with Mexican Indians. He is married to a consecrated companion, and hand in hand

they are doing what they believe is God's will. A graduate of
Texas Western College in El Paso, Texas, he went into Home
Mission work with the Tairra Maiija Indians who live in
three gigantic canyons deep in the state of Chihuahua, Mex-
ico. They are totally primitive. Many still wear breech cloth.
Their diet is 80 percent corn. Fewer than one half of their
children live to age ten. Their poverty is indescribable.

In an effort to create an understandable language Don has
joined himself to the Wycliffe Translators. He builds a language by listening to the Indians speak, then writes the
language, using the New Testament to teach the people to
read. Churches have sprung up by giving the people the
Bible in a form they can read. Don has no stated salary.
People in the United States support him privately, but out of
his income he must send 11 percent to the Wycliffe Translators. They are putting aside nothing and have no provision
for retirement. They are accumulating nothing in the way of
things, yet they are radiantly happy. They have forgotten
self, losing themselves in the service of living abundantly
spiritually.

Walking down the street one day I was impressed by a
sign: "CAFETERIA. Serve yourself and save." There is a significant message in this subline. If we could only realize that
much which we are privileged to give comes back to us in
unrealized blessings!

Serve yourself and you save. Nothing is truer. For the
things you gain by your own efforts stay by you and become
a large part of you. Yet you may keep giving away what you
have accumulated and still be rich. There are those who are
so afraid they will do something for themselves that they are
unable to do anything for anyone else. The millionaire who
delights in giving to worthy causes first had to get the wealth
himself. But there is the other side. When you serve and

share with someone else, you always serve yourself. You have a loyal friend in whom there is a world of wealth—an intermixture of faith, inspiration, and love. Lighten your neighbor's load, and you will receive more than you give. Life becomes abundantly rewarding.

Worshiping with some friends of the Methodist church on the day of observance of the Lord's Supper, we were greatly impressed by a statement of the minister as each group of communicants was ready to leave the altar rail. After quoting a suitable Scripture verse, he would say: "Arise, and go in peace, and may your abundant life in Christ overflow in deeds of love and service."

The motto of the Future Farmers of America is:

Learning to Do,
Doing to Learn;
Earning to Live,
Living to Serve.

May we take these two keys of *love* and *service* as patterns for all of life's days.

5
Going God's Way

To every man there openeth
A Way, and Ways, and a Way,
And the High Soul climbs the High Way,
And the Low Soul gropes the Low;
And in between, on the misty flats,
The rest drift to and fro.
But to every man there openeth
A High Way and a Low,
And every man decideth
The way his soul shall go.[1]

The message of this poem is crystal clear. From time to time every person faces a great decision. Every day is filled with the apparently small choices. Ultimately a person faces the enormous choices and discovers anew Markham's insistence that "choices are the hinges of destiny." These choices, these decisions will determine the *Way* he will go in life.

From the beginning of time this has been true. Adam and Eve faced a choice and their decision brought sin into the world. Today much of the world does not know God, and

---

[1] "The Ways," John Oxenham. Permission of Miss Theo Dunkerley, High Salvington, Worthing, England.

many who have heard his word, like Adam, are running away from God. They are unwilling to follow Christ and his pattern for life.

How often have we heard an individual say, "But I had no other choice." In answer to a question put by the television announcer to an FBI agent, "Have you ever had to kill a man?" he replied: "No, and I have seen only one man killed by our agents, and we had no choice. He reached for his gun and we had to let him have it."

We may get lots of conversation about the Oriental monkey trio with hands appropriately placed over their eyes, ears, and mouth to depict the phrases, "See no evil, speak no evil, hear no evil." But the other side of this simple idea is followed by all too many people: "See no good, speak no good, hear no good." God has given man the freedom of choice between good and evil, between acceptance or rejection of him. This choice leaves no room for neutrality. "No man can serve two masters: for either he will hate the one, and love the other; or else he will hold to the one, and despise the other. Ye cannot serve God and mammon" (Matt. 6:24).

The choice is ours. We must *look* and *talk* and *listen* and be actively engaged in the search for more understanding of God and of "going his way."

In the early days of Jesus' ministry he spoke to the multitudes the message which has come down through the ages, known as the Sermon on the Mount. The concluding section of this sermon is of an intensely solemn character. Things and persons are brought face to face with immediate and eternal issues of life. Jesus is giving us a comparison of what we may expect if we take the wrong road or the wrong gate—the High Road or the Low Road. He tells us plainly that the end will be everlasting life or destruction.

Note how definite he is as he makes the distinction: "Enter ye in at the strait gate: for wide is the gate, and broad is the way, that leadeth to destruction, and many there be which go in thereat: because strait is the gate, and *narrow is the way*, which leadeth unto life, and few there be that find it" (Matt. 7:13–14).

Years before the coming of our Saviour, God had spoken through the prophet Isaiah, warning the people of the folly of not going his way:

Let the wicked forsake his way, and the unrighteous man his thoughts: and let him return unto the Lord, and he will have mercy upon him; and to our God, for he will abundantly pardon. For my thoughts are not your thoughts, neither are *your ways my ways*, saith the Lord. For as the heavens are higher than the earth, *so are my ways* higher than your ways, and my thoughts than your thoughts (55:7–9).

Throughout the Psalms there runs a golden thread of the psalmist's admonition that only God's way is the High Road to a life of happiness and blessing to others. From the very first line of these heartwarming messages this is noted: "Blessed is the man that *walketh not* in the counsel of the ungodly, nor standeth in the *way* of sinners, nor sitteth in the seat of the scornful. . . . For the Lord knoweth *the way* of the righteous: but the *way of the ungodly* shall perish (1:1–6).

Life is full of pitfalls, of muddy and worn roads; and it should be a constant challenge to everyone to seek the better way of life. Yes, the High Road. We should not let the fact that we may have traveled over some bad highways in our personal life hinder us from seeking the better way in the future. We should decide to go farther than we have ever gone before in everything we undertake to do. We should set a better pace, attain a higher goal, because as the poet has said, "The High Soul climbs the High Way . . . And every man decideth/The way his soul shall go."

Again we go to the psalmist and find him hungering and thirsting for the better way:

Teach me thy way, O Lord; I will walk in thy truth: unite my heart to fear thy name (86:11).

Teach me, O Lord, the way of thy statutes; and I shall keep it unto the end. Give me understanding, and I shall keep thy law; yea, I shall observe it with my whole heart (119:33–34).

Likewise, the writer of Proverbs warns us that man must not depend upon his own judgment to know the way of life:

Trust in the Lord with all thine heart; and lean not unto thine own understanding. In *all thy ways* acknowledge him, and he shall direct thy paths (3:5–6).

There is a way which seemeth right unto a man, but the end thereof are the ways of death. . . . A wise man feareth, and departeth from evil: but the fool rageth, and is confident (14:12–16).

Throughout the world there is hunger for a better way of life, particularly in so many of the undeveloped countries. Much of our Government's foreign aid is intended to be used in improving the agricultural, manufacturing, health, and economic conditions of the people. Better standards of living is the goal of those in leadership and in the administration of these gifts and loans to governments of other lands. Much of this work is being undertaken by the Peace Corps. Unfortunately, all too much of this aid is being sidetracked by corrupt officials into their own personal channels and for their own personal gain.

Here in our own favored country, there is a constant effort to find a better way to do so many things. Scientists are constantly striving to find, through the use of chemicals, electronics, and various types of building materials, a way of improving the welfare of mankind. Great strides have been made. Much of industry has been modernized through automation and electronic equipment, all of which is for a better way of life and better working conditions.

Look for a moment at the field of medicine. Some sixty years ago a young man wanted to find his place of service. He began his preparation for the ministry, but this did not seem to be God's will for his life; so he turned to medicine. Again the future looked dark. His practice was slow; patients did not come, but he was not discouraged. Using his spare time, he read all the medical journals and became obsessed with the tragedies he witnessed in the disease called diabetes, which was making people waste away.

In the summer of 1921 he was able to borrow a laboratory when students were not using it. He received little encouragement from friends, but he toiled away at his complex experiments. At last his efforts were rewarded in the discovery of insulin. Two years later, in 1923, Sir Frederick Grant Banting was made professor of medical research in his own University of Toronto and was awarded one of the coveted Nobel prizes in recognition of his tireless efforts.

There are still so many opportunities for medical and scientific workers as they search for a cure for cancer and for the reduction of heart disease. Today there are thousands of people who owe their life to the patient and humble research already done. We can only utter words of praise and appreciation for these men who were rewarded for their efforts.

There are still other fields of service in which godly men are needed. When are we going to turn our thoughts and attention to the higher values of life, to the spiritual values which Christ taught?

It was a momentous day in the history of the world, September 2, 1945, when General Douglas MacArthur stood on the deck of the battleship *Missouri* to accept the Japanese surrender. After a brief statement to the assembled representatives of the Allied Powers and the signing of the documents of surrender, MacArthur spoke to the American people. His heart swelled with pride, but there was a deep sense of humility as he foresaw even further sacrifices in the years ahead as ways would be sought for a lasting peace. Challenging were his words as he almost pled for a more determined dedication for Christians, and even non-Christians, to walk God's way, and for a revitalization of the spiritual values of life.

Men since the beginning of time have sought peace. Various methods through the ages have attempted to devise an international process to prevent or settle disputes between nations. From the very start workable methods were found insofar as individual citizens were concerned, but the mechanics of an instrumentality of larger international scope have never been successful. Military alliances, balances of power, leagues of nations, all in turn failed, leaving the only path to be by way of the crucible of war. We have had our last chance. If we do not now devise some greater and more equitable system, Armageddon will be at our door. The *problem basically is theological and involves a spiritual recrudescence and improvement of human character* that will synchronize with our almost matchless advances in science, art, literature and all material and cultural developments of the past two thousand years. It must be of the spirit if we are to save the flesh.[2]

---

[2] Douglas MacArthur, *Reminiscences* (New York: McGraw-Hill Book Co., 1964), p. 276. Used by permission.

It was a solemn hour as Jesus and his disciples sat together around the table in a secluded room the night of his betrayal. He was trying to prepare them for what was ahead. As kindly as he knew how, he said that he would leave them, going to prepare a place for them in his Father's home, and that he would come again to take them to be with him. "You know the way," he said. Thomas interrupted, saying, "We don't know where you are going; how can we know the way?" Jesus answered, "I am the way, the truth, and the life. No man cometh to the Father but by me. If you had known me, ye should have known my Father also." Philip interrupted, asking that they be shown the Father, and they would be satisfied. How patiently Jesus answered him! "Have I been so long time with you, and hast thou not known me, Philip? He that hath seen me hath seen the Father." The message is clear: the way to God is Jesus Christ. God sent his Son into the world to reveal himself to all mankind, to show men "God's way."

What we now call Christianity was first known by the very way in which Jesus had spoken of himself—"the way." It designated the followers of Jesus.

"Way" is a common, often inconspicuous word in modern speech, especially in connection with modes of travel. Because we constantly need directions to go where we want to go, we rely on highway maps, or consult airlines as to the best route. Over and over again we may ask, "Is this the way?"

In spiritual values, the sum of all our little ways and byways adds up to our way of life. What kind of way is it? The supreme way of all life is God's way: love, understanding, forgiveness, patience, neighborliness, all leading to eternal life. All other ways lead to death.

When God's way and man's way diverge, it is always

because man goes his own way without God. God, however, has chosen to go *his way* with man. *His way* has been made known to us, especially in Christ, and he expects us to make it known to others. His presence in any man becomes a challenge of salvation to every other man.

So the way is clear. We need only the will to follow it. This is why the Master taught his disciples to pray: "Thy kingdom come. Thy will be done." As the psalmist prayed, he said: "God be merciful unto us, and bless us; and cause his face to shine upon us; that *thy way* may be known upon earth, thy saving health among all nations" (67:1–2).

6
A Purpose to Live For

During the sunset years of his life, Dr. Rufus Jones, who for so many years taught at Haverford College, Haverford, Pennsylvania, confided to some of his intimate friends one of the guiding purposes of his life as he tried to influence the young men with whom he came in contact. God had been good to give to Dr. and Mrs. Jones a lovely lad to whom they were greatly devoted, and who for eleven years had been the joy of their life. Then in his providence God had called the lad home to be with him.

In his study at Haverford College, Dr. Jones had many photographs of distinguished personalities, but in the center of the mantel was the portrait of his boy Lowell. After the lad's death, Dr. Jones said: "I overheard him once talking with a group of his playmates, when each was telling what he wanted to be when he grew up. When his turn came, Lowell said, 'I want to grow up to be a man like my daddy.' Few things in my life have given me a greater impulse to dedication. What kind of man was I going to be, if I was to be the pattern for my boy?" Dr. Jones never lost faith with his boy, never lost the master motive of his life.

When Lucius Annaeus Seneca was falsely accused by

Nero of a conspiracy against him, he was ordered to take his own life. Turning to his weeping family and friends, he gently reminded them that they must accept with courage that which it was not in their power to control. Refused the right to make a will, he said he would leave them the best thing he had: *the pattern of his life.*

Who is going to be the pattern for your life? Every thoughtful person is now and then tantalized by the question, "What is my real purpose in life?" When we find what we believe to be the correct answer to this, another question nibbles at our conscience: "Is this really what I should want out of life?" Man needs a purpose in life. It is not how long a man lives but how well he lives. Individuals who have no purpose have little peace in life. They are forever vacillating to and fro. God's greatest gift to man is to help him to be something.

Life is a progressive achievement. There must be growth or stagnation. Look at the long years of study and preparation for a young doctor, and even after he is ready for practice, there must be continued study and observation of the new techniques in the medical field. So it is with the Christian, especially young church members. They must grow. Billy Graham always stresses a follow-up campaign for the new Christians.

The life of the apostle Paul should be a challenge to every thoughtful Christian. In the closing years of his life, in humility and honesty he made no claim to personal perfection or to complete knowledge of Christ, but dramatically he wrote: "Brethren, I count not myself to have apprehended: but this one thing I do, forgetting those things which are behind, and reaching forth unto those things which are before, I press toward the mark for the prize of the high calling of God in Christ Jesus" (Phil. 3:13–14).

What a noble purpose for living! What a master motive for one's life! What a glorious goal for all us Christians to try to achieve!

Our God is a God of purpose. He has a purpose for you and for me. There is joy in his heart when we do his will, when we follow his leading. God had a purpose for his servants of old. Speaking to Abraham, as recorded in Genesis 12, he said: "Get thee out of thy country, and from thy kindred, and from thy father's house, unto a land that I will shew thee: . . . And I will bless them that bless thee, and curse him that curseth thee: and in thee shall all families of the earth be blessed" (vv. 1–3).

Note that God was specific in his statement that he would bless Abraham and all his families if he followed his guiding hand. We will observe the same promise in the case of other servants of God.

Greatly concerned as to the welfare of his children and their great persecution by Pharaoh in Egypt, God called Moses at the burning bush: "Come now therefore, and I will send thee unto Pharaoh, that thou mayest bring forth my people the children of Israel out of Egypt. . . . And he said, Certainly I will be with thee" (Ex. 3:10–12).

Moses followed God's leadership with the children of Israel, but in the providence of God he was not permitted to lead them into the Land of Promise. God had another man ready, a man with a purpose to be fulfilled. And God spoke to Joshua, saying: "Moses my servant is dead; now therefore arise, go over this Jordan, thou, and all this people, unto the land which I do give to them, even to the children of Israel. . . . As I was with Moses, so I will be with thee: I will not fail thee, nor forsake thee. . . . Be strong and of a good courage" (Josh. 1:2–6).

Always God was standing by to give guidance and protection to the men he had chosen to fulfil a mission on earth.

There is not a more beautiful and dramatic story in all literature than that of Joseph. The evidence of God's purpose for Joseph is so beautifully portrayed when, as governor of Egypt, Joseph makes himself known to his brothers: "Now therefore be not grieved, nor angry with yourselves, that ye sold me hither: for God did send me before you to preserve life. . . . God sent me before you to preserve you a posterity in the earth, and to save your lives by a great deliverance" (Gen. 45:5–7).

It cannot be said that any of these servants failed in their mission. It was a rebellious and ungrateful people who failed to heed God's admonitions, his call to a higher and nobler way of living. But God did not turn his back on the peoples of the world. As one great act of love and compassion he sent his beloved Son in a further effort to redeem a lost world. Jesus came with a mission to be fulfilled, with a purpose to live and to die for. The scribes and Pharisees conspired with Pilate and the Roman authorities to thwart the purpose of Jesus as they sent him to the cross. After the crucifixion, they thought they had securely sealed him in a tomb. They were determined to get him out of their way because he was hindering their way of life. But God's will, God's purpose for the world cannot be sealed in a Roman tomb. And God's will for your life, and mine, cannot be frustrated if we give ourselves wholeheartedly to his way of life.

Regardless of how successful one may be in life, the greatest achievement, the greatest happiness, the greatest security will only come from the overmastering purpose of living in the will of God, in striving and pressing forward toward the prize of the high calling of God in Christ Jesus. Over and over again we get this lesson from Jesus himself. On his lips continually were words like these, in which he endeavored

in every instance to stress his sense of mission and purpose—that of doing his Father's will:

I must work the works of him that sent me, while it is day: the
night cometh, when no man can work (John 9:4).

The thief cometh not, but for to steal, and to kill, and to
destroy: I am come that they might have life, and that they
might have it more abundantly (10:10).

Other sheep I have, which are not of this fold: them also I must
bring, and they shall hear my voice; and there shall be one fold,
and one shepherd (v. 16).

As you seek to do the will of God, does your life have a
commanding center? Are Christ and his teaching the domi-
nating purpose in your life? Until we have one loyalty to
which we give obedience over all other calls, we are divided
persons. "Life is very simple," said Madame Chiang Kai-
shek, "and yet how confused we make it seem. In old
Chinese art there is in each picture only one outstanding
object. Everything else is subordinated to that one beauti-
fying thing. An integrated life is like that. What is the one
beautiful flower? As I feel it now, it is doing the will of God.
I used to pray that God would do this or that. Now I pray
only that God will make his will known to me."

Are you willing to do his will? Are we willing to have one
master purpose in life? Would it be worth his time to reveal
his will for us? It is a great moment in human personality
when a man says sincerely, "I want to do God's will, not my
own!" To make this resolve a realization, there must be a
beginning.

A traveler once asked Socrates, "How can I reach Mount
Olympus?" The discerning philosopher replied: "*Just make
every step you take go in that direction.*" It was a good
answer for climbing a mountain or for building a life of

dedication. Have you taken that first step? Have you made a beginning? Have you set for yourself a master motive—a master purpose to live for? If not, I challenge you to make this prayer by Percy R. Hayward your prayer:

Thou God of far-distant purposes, I pray thee, set in my mind now some goal in the future for which to live.

Save me from narrowing absorption in that which is here and now.

Ennoble and empower me with a clear picture of that which lies far ahead.

Set before me the kind of person I am yet to be. Grant me to see something of the work I am to do. Hang thou on the walls of my mind now the home I am to have in the years to come.

Show me the wisdom I am to make my own, the place I am to fill in making thy will effective in our world. Let some of what is out yonder in the years-to-be come and abide in my heart now.

So may that distant goal, O God, steady me in the difficult journey of today.

And enable thou the thoughts and acts of my present life to be shaped by the demands of that unattained purpose.[1]

"By faith Moses, when he was grown up, refused to be called the son of Pharaoh's daughter; choosing rather to share illtreatment with the people of God, than to enjoy the pleasures of sin for a season" (Heb. 11:24–25, ASV).

---

[1] Percy R. Hayward, *Young People's Prayers* (New York: Association Press, 1950), p. 36. Used by permission.

7
Life Is a Trust

In mid-September, members of the Jewish faith in every community inaugurate a ten-day period known as High Holy Days. Rosh Hashanah is their New Year, or the opening day of special services. It is celebrated as the birthday of the world and mankind. Yom Kippur, the closing day of the special observance, is the Day of Atonement. In explaining this season of special emphases, Rabbi Jerome Kestenbaum of the West End Synagogue, Nashville, Tennessee, said in a TV interview: "It is a universal holiday at which time we pray for all humanity. Our aspirations and hopes for a world in which peace, justice, and liberty will reign supreme, and the inherent dignity of the human being will be respected." Announcing a series of ten sermons, "What Counts Most in Life," he closed the interview with the challenging statement, *"Our life is God's gift to us. What we do with it is our gift to him."* In other words, our life is a trust. What will we do with it? What will be our guiding principles as we live from day to day?

The apostle Paul demonstrated the conviction that he had a mission in life, that his life was a gift from God, and that as a steward he must acknowledge his trusteeship? Paul did not always have this spirit of dedication, but after he met Christ on the Damascus road he was a new man. Note the affirmation of his dedication, the pattern of his life's purpose: "For though I preach the gospel, I have nothing to glory of: for necessity is laid upon me; yea, woe is unto me, if I preach not the gospel!" (1 Cor. 9:16).

As a human being one has the choice of three basic attitudes toward life. He may approach life with the philosophy of the turnip, in which case his life will consist of being born, eating, drinking, sleeping, maturing, mating, growing old, and dying.

The second basic attitude is to look at life as if it were a business. A great many so-called successful men and women believe life is a business, and they arrange their conduct and behavior accordingly. If you believe that life is a business, your first question of life, naturally, is, "What do I get out of it?" and your first reaction to any new experience is, "How much is it worth to me?"

The third attitude toward life is the approach of the artist. Here the underlying philosophy is "What can I put into it?" and the basic relation of the individual to his fellowmen is one of cooperation and common sense. History remembers best those who have contributed most richly to the welfare of their fellowmen. When God measures a man, he puts the tape around the heart instead of the head. "Keep thy heart with all diligence; for out of it are the issues of life" (Prov. 4:23).

Existence is given us all to start with; our problem is somehow to make life out of existence. Existence is an instrument; life is an achievement. Now all human experience agrees that real life, real happiness, can only come when a worthy purpose runs down through the center of existence to give it meaning. Life must be recognized as "a trust" from

God, and our stewardship must be faithfully fulfilled. Amid the infinite variety of daily experiences, one attribute is always present when a great man stands out in a community. He has centered his existence around some worthy aim, concerning which he feels like Paul, "This one thing I do."

As one goes forth to the work and duties of the day, busy with many things, tangible and material, may we be ever mindful that we are here to further the kingdom of our Lord and Saviour. May the task of earning a living not claim our whole thought and enterprise. May we learn from Jesus that the only greatness comes of a willingness to serve.

> A charge to keep I have,
> A God to glorify,
> Who gave His Son my soul to save,
> And fit it for the sky.
>
> To serve the present age,
> My calling to fulfill;
> O may it all my pow'rs engage
> To do my Master's will!
>
> Arm me with jealous care,
> As in Thy sight to live;
> And O Thy servant, Lord, prepare
> A strict account to give.

A disturbing approach to life was brought out by the prosecution in the trial of three men for the kidnaping of Frank Sinatra, Jr., December 28, 1963. A letter, found in the lockbox of one of the kidnapers, was addressed to his parents and loved ones:

If you read this letter, I am either dead or under arrest for felony kidnapping. If I am convicted . . . I will be in prison for at least ten years.

Why? As you all know, money has always been of utmost importance to me. . . .

After realizing that I was incapable of earning enough money to keep up with all my debts and high living I decided to take a carefully calculated risk by undertaking a major crime. If I had succeeded I would net approximately $100,000 which would have enabled me to become a millionaire in ten or fifteen years. . . .

I rationalized that working to accumulate enough money to ever be able to approach becoming wealthy, I would have to earn around $300,000 annually—a very optimistic earning projection—for about fifteen years, saving most of my untapped earnings and passing up the temptation of living in luxury. . . . I believe I would have lived it up . . . so about three months ago I started thinking of a crime that would involve few people and return much money. Kidnapping seemed to offer the least risk for the money, so I set to work planning a perfect crime. Naturally, if you are reading this, the crime was unperfect. . . .

On and on the young man continued as to how he would spend the money. He would give his parents many of the things they had never had. He would remember his friends with lavish Christmas presents. He even said in the letter, "I also made a promise to God that I would pay back the money to the church and special charities as rapidly as possible." What he meant by "pay back" is not understandable. One may interpret this as a guilty conscience for having neglected his duty to God in years gone by. He expressed regret for the heartaches which he knew his parents would suffer because of this reckless deed, and closed by saying, "I hope God will help us all through the problems of life. We all should try to help ourselves to happiness that life can provide."

How can one expect happiness with God left out? How can

one expect happiness when the accumulation of *things* is the master motive, the driving power of one's life? "Things" just do not satisfy. Today this young man, the victim of the urge for money, has been sentenced to jail for life, plus seventy-five years.

In contrast to the tragic conception of life as displayed by a young man just twenty-three years old, let's look at another individual, a missionary to China, dedicated and devoted to the belief that "life is a trust."

Shortly before China fell to the Communists, Bob Pierce of World Vision arrived late one night in Shanghai where he had reserved a room in the China Inland Mission quarters. A note by the dim bulb burning in the vestibule said that since the compound was filled with guests that night everyone had to share a room. Tiptoeing upstairs he found his room and prepared for bed in the dark so as not to disturb his roommate. Reclining and pondering the day's activities, he was startled by the sobbing of the man in the next cot. Thinking the man was dreaming, Pierce said nothing. But after fifteen minutes of sobbing he said, "Friend, I don't know you. And I guess you don't know me. But whatever the trouble is, I wish you would share it with me. The Bible says we're to bear one another's burdens."

The man told his story. Twenty-one years before he and his bride had come as missionaries from the United States. They had asked to be assigned, not to a city along the China coast, but to some difficult inland place where few others would dare to go. They were sent to the Tibetan borders, as far from civilization as a person could get. It took them four months to reach the field. Once every three years the missionary and his wife would return to the China coast for a physical checkup and to replenish dwindling supplies.

Pierce could almost feel the loneliness and privation of such an existence. But the man said they didn't mind those things. They worked seven years without a convert, even though they had learned the language. In the seventh year God gave them a tiny baby which he helped bring into the world with his own rough hands. The Tibetans took a "shine" to the growing baby, showing her a fondness never given the parents. She learned Tibetan as easily as the national children. Verses her parents taught her she in turn taught the Tibetan children. When reaching the Tibetans had seemed hopeless, the first convert was won through the instrumentality of the little girl. Now there were eight converts. Twenty-one years had been spent to show eight people the way to eternal life.

The man paused, then went on. "As I talk to you now, my wife and fourteen-year-old daughter are sailing down the river to the Pacific Ocean. They're on their way home to America."

Pierce asked, "If they're going home, why don't you go too? If it's lack of funds I'll wire America tonight. I know churches would send you the money to fly home so you could meet your family at the dock. Twenty-one years is long enough for one man to serve. Let somebody else take over!"

The missionary replied, "What about the eight converts? They're young in Christ, struggling in a godless environment. They need guidance. It would be years before anyone else could learn the language. No, I must return. Tomorrow morning I'm heading back for three more years."

Then he told Pierce the reason for the separation. "For more than a year there has been a numbness in my daughter's arm. When we brought her to Shanghai for medical attention last week the doctor took me aside to give me the verdict. That girl God gave us on the mission field has contracted leprosy."

The next morning Pierce saw him heading for the borders of Tibet for another three years, all alone. He was willing to give up family and furlough and ease in grateful dedication of life to him who left his heavenly home in the ivory palaces for the rigors of a hostile world.[1]

---

[1] Leslie B. Flynn, *Did I Say Thanks?* (Nashville: Broadman Press, 1963), pp. 104–106.

Life is a trust. The apostle Paul knew this when he said: "For to me to live is Christ, and to die is gain" (Phil. 1:21). Paul had tied his life up with Christ. "Mainspring and motive of all obedience and holiness is thankful response to love divine. The love of Christ for us should constrain us to such appreciation that we cannot but live for him who died for us. The first gift a grateful Christian should make is himself. Our life should be a constant stanza of thankful service: steadfast, unmovable, always abounding in the work of the Lord." [2]

> Lord, make me an instrument of Thy peace.
> Where there is hate, may I bring love;
> Where offense, may I bring pardon;
> May I bring union in place of discord;
> Truth, replacing error;
> Faith, where once there was doubt;
> Hope, for despair;
> Light, where was darkness;
> Joy to replace sadness.
> Make me not to so crave to be loved as to love.
> Help me to learn that in giving I may receive;
> In forgetting self, I may find life eternal.
>
> —*Francis of Assisi*

---

[2] *Ibid.*, p. 106.

8
Life's Three Dimensions

God is the master architect of the universe. He would like to be the architect of every human life. Our span of life was meant for lofty duties, not for selfishness; not to be whiled away for aimless dreams, but to improve ourselves and serve mankind. Hans Christian Andersen, the writer of so many fascinating stories for children, has said: "Every man's life is like a fairy tale, written by God's fingers." Would that all men could be led to place their hands in God's hands and let him lead them into a life of abundant living.

The building of a life which will serve mankind, like the erection of a great physical structure for commercial uses, or the building of a great cathedral for the worship of God, must be well planned. An architect is an integral part, in fact a necessity, if these structures are to be of lasting value. The blue prints and pages of specifications are the architect's patterns for the erection of the building.

When God planned the building of the tabernacle as recorded so minutely in Exodus 24–26, three dimensions recur like a great refrain—length, depth, and height. These dimensions were applied to every phase of the structure and to the materials to be used.

Life, too, is characterized by these three dimensions. We are necessarily restricted in the length of our life by heredity and accidental factors beyond our control, yet modern science and medical research have greatly lengthened life's span. It is not at all uncommon to know, and to hear of, individuals who have lived far beyond threescore and ten, and even fourscore years. The great humanitarian, former President Herbert Hoover, who did so much for the hungry people of the world, and General Douglas MacArthur, both lived to the ripe ages of ninety. And the great football player and coach, Alonzo Stagg, lived to one hundred two. A Negro slave of our city died in 1966 at the age of one hundred twelve, and we have a dear neighbor, probably in his last illness, who is ninety-six.

While we cannot control the *length* of our life, we should certainly discipline ourselves in many areas of daily living whereby we may prolong life. A United States Public Health Service report has revealed that more than 12 percent of this country's people are limited in their activities because of chronic disease or impairment. Heart conditions, arthritis, and rheumatism lead to the various causes that keep 22.2 million people from working. And as might be expected, the ability to get around and work or play decreases with a man's age.

Granted, we cannot control the length of our life, but each of us can exert a great impact and influence on the other two dimensions, breadth and height.

There is no life so humble, if it be true and genuinely human and obedient to God, that it may not hope to shed some of his light. There is no life so meager that the greatest and wisest of us can afford to despise it. We cannot know at what moment it may flash forth with the life of God. Thomas G. Huxley said: "The rung of a ladder was never meant to rest upon, but only to hold man's foot long enough to enable him to put the other somewhat higher."

To reach the full dimensions of either height or depth, there must be another ingredient, breadth. Breadth involves a sense of wholehearted dedication to our particular specialized calling. It also implies a broad interest in other fields of endeavor. This brings the necessity of development and discipline.

Height is attained by lifting one's spirit and soul unto God and by giving service to others. We live in deeds and not in years.

During one's lifetime a person's importance may be evaluated by the number of people who serve him, but after his death a different yardstick applies.

Napoleon made himself master of France and most of Europe by the power of his marching legions, while Louis Pasteur made himself the servant of France, and of the world, by fighting the germs and diseases. The serving of Pasteur outlives Napoleon.

Mussolini dominated Italy for a decade; Marconi put his electrical wizardry at the services of the nation and the world. Only his efforts still benefit his fellowman.[1]

Hitler and Stalin both had a sadistic conception of life. Their names will forever go down in history in disrepute. Communism is dedicated to destroy the dignity of man. Its philosophy is entirely anti-Christ and anti-everything for which he stood and for which he died that we might have eternal life.

James and John came to Jesus and asked, "Master, we would that thou shouldest do for us whatsoever we shall

---

[1] World Religious News, *Guideposts*, May, 1965, p. 6. Used by permission.

desire. And he said unto them, "What would ye that I should do for you?" We know the rest of the story. Out of their greed and selfishness they wanted to sit on each side of him in glory. They were interested only in themselves. Jesus was quick to answer that this was not in keeping with everything that he had been trying to teach them. It is a simple lesson but hard to learn. It is the mark of true greatness. "Whosoever will be great among you, shall be your minister: And whosoever of you will be the chiefest, shall be servant of all. For even the Son of man came not to be ministered unto, but to minister, and to give his life a ransom for many" (Mark 10:43–45).

In the twentieth century, one man stands head and shoulders above others as its greatest humanitarian and servant. He has had his critics, but we are yet to see any of them match him as a model of sacrificial service. Not only did he have great length of life, but its breadth and depth and height are a challenge to every noble man and woman. I refer to Dr. Albert Schweitzer. His pattern of life is a worthy example for all who would be of service to mankind, no matter what their religion.

He was criticized for many of his foibles and old-fashioned habits. Many of his religious beliefs have also been questioned, yet at heart he was God's servant to the core. His philosophy was *reverence for life*. Visited by *Life* magazine correspondent Hugh Moffett, he was asked this question: "Can you find any cause for optimism in the world today?"

" 'Optimism!' he exclaimed. 'How can I speak of optimism when Africa is in the state it is? How can you speak of optimism for the rest of the world? It is a difficult time for the world. It is necessary for the men involved to be clear and strong in their leadership.

" 'There is help for Africa, as other places, in the word of

Jesus in the New Testament: there is always water to cleanse.' " [2]

Continuing their conversation, the columnist asked, "Which of your many achievements are you proudest of?"

" 'Proud? I am not proud. . . . The greatest satisfaction is in the healing of the people. . . . After all I came here to put religion into practice. Christianity will propagate only when put into practice. . . . It is not to say that I have not taken satisfaction. Let us say that I am happy to have come here and to have done what we have done. But I think everyone should do some work for the coming of the Kingdom. We all should have the Spirit of Christ. Thanks to the Gospel, which tells us of the life of Christ, we can all be in contact with Him.' " [3]

There is a place of service for all mankind. It is our mission to find it.

The Harder Task

Teach me to Live! 'Tis easier far to die—
  Gently and silently to pass away—
On earth's long night to close the heavy eye,
  And waken in the glorious realms of day.

Teach me that harder lesson—how to live
  To serve Thee in the darkest paths of life.
Arm me for conflict, now fresh vigor give,
  And make me more than conqu'ror in the strife.

—*Author Unknown*

---

[2] Hugh Moffett, "The White Wizard's 90th," *Life,* February 19, 1965, p. 92. Used by permission.
[3] *Ibid.*

9
Life's Compensations

"And the Lord God formed man of the dust of the ground, and breathed into his nostrils the breath of life; and man became a living soul" (Gen. 2:7).

Life is the most precious gift man can have, but we all too often make provisions for this life as if it were never to have an end, and for the other life as though it were never to have a beginning. We are living in an age such as few periods of the world's history have even witnessed. Never has there been so much greed, so much struggling for the accumulation of earthly possessions. Jesus warned against this pattern of life when he said: "For what shall it profit a man, if he shall gain the whole world, and lose his own soul? Or what shall a man give in exchange for his soul? Whosoever therefore shall be ashamed of me and my words in this adulterous and sinful generation; of him also shall the Son of man be ashamed, when he cometh in the glory of his Father with the holy angels" (Mark 8:36–38).

In his book *Wind, Sand and Stars*, Antoine de Saint-Exupéry, for many years a French aviator, relates many of his flying experiences during his world travels and his participation in the Spanish Civil War. Writing about this war, Antoine relates a most gripping story of a little company of soldiers. They sat one night in a subterranean chamber on the Madrid front, eating their evening meal. The telephone rang and the captain received an order to attack at daybreak an entrenched area of some twenty houses in an industrial district only a short distance away. There would be little support for this little group and it would be a very dangerous mission. Turning to Sergeant X, he said: "Sergeant, you will lead the attack with me. Go get some sleep."

Every man in the room knew that Sergeant X had a date with death. That night he went to bed fully dressed, his whole body covered with the tools of his trade—cartridge belt, hand grenades, and his rifle by his side. His was a restless night as he lay on his iron cot in a little workman's house, around which trenches had been dug.

During the night, unknown to him, or to any of the other soldiers, an order had come through canceling the attack. At sunrise, the soldiers awakened. Sergeant X, sleepy-eyed, jumped to his feet, grabbed his rifle, and shouted, "Captain, are we off?"

Gathering the group together to make an announcement, the captain said: "The attack has been called off."

After the men had gained their composure, the captain walked over to the Sergeant and put his hand on his shoulder, and said: "Sergeant, let me tell you that we have made you a present of your life. Just that. As much as if you had stood at the foot of the electric chair. And God knows, the world sheds ink enough on the pathos of pardon at the foot of the electric chair. We brought you your pardon *in extremis*. No question about it. In your mind there was nothing between you and death but a thickness of tissue-paper. . . . Sergeant, Sergeant, what will you do with this gift of life?" [1]

Life is fraught with so many responsibilities, so many

---

[1] (New York: Harcourt, Brace & World, Inc., 1939), pp. 282–83.

opportunities, so many blessings, so many avenues of service, and so many compensations, other than the material things of life. Frances Anne Kemble in "The Burden" says:

> A sacred burden in this life we bear,
> Look on it, lift it, bear it solemnly,
> Stand up and walk beneath it steadfastly;
> Fail not for sorrow, falter not for sin,
> But onward, upward, till the goal we win.

This span of life was meant for lofty duties, not for selfishness; not to be whiled away by aimless dreams, but to improve ourselves and serve mankind. And there are so many ways in which this can be done, yet we are tempted to fritter away our days trying to "keep up with the Joneses," trying to accumulate the paltry things of this world.

Mrs. Martha Imhoff, of Williamsport, Massachusetts, has written:

The other day I watched a little boy throw a tantrum in a store. He wanted a dump truck; his mother refused. Junior howled louder and louder until the mother, embarrassed, bought the toy.

As I watched this scene I thought of my mother and her advice to me when I was young. "Martha," she would say, "don't hang your heart on things."

When there was a particular dress I craved in a store window my mother would talk about the joy that comes with looking at things without always wanting them. I'll admit there were times when I rebelled against this philosophy, but today as I see what materialism can do for people, I'm grateful for her early teaching. It's a motto that I think should hang in every home: "Don't hang your heart on things." [2]

---

[2] *Guideposts*, May, 1965, p. 10. Used by permission.

There are values in life far more rewarding than things. There are compensations which money cannot buy.

Jesus was speaking of the true use of life in the verses we have already quoted from Mark. In the two previous verses (Mark 8:34–35), he stressed even more strongly the importance of unselfish living: "Whosoever will come after me, let him deny himself, and take up his cross, and follow me. For whosoever will save his life shall lose it; but whosoever shall lose his life for my sake and the gospel's, the same shall save it."

One of the most "attention-getting" advertisements I think I ever saw was in the issue of *Look* magazine, October 18, 1966. It was an ad of the Equitable Life Assurance Society. Silhouetted against a black background was a modest home. The house was dark except for a light in one window. Through this window one could see the father, in his shirt sleeves, seated at a table, intently studying some papers. The lead line of the ad read: "Some men forget time when it comes to helping others." Listing several of their successful agents, the writer of the ad said further: "They are all devoted to their work. Dedicated to their client's welfare. Because they give much of themselves to others, the rewards they get in return are great." Yes, rewards not so much in commissions or salaries, but the inner satisfaction of having helped fathers and husbands anticipate the needs of their loved ones in the event their earning power should be interrupted, or death should overtake them.

A mother of six children was sick for two years. Therefore, the eldest child, Jean, was up at five o'clock several mornings each week to help her mother before leaving for work. She set aside evenings for the housework her mother could not do. Jean was getting so thin that several of her associates became anxious about her. "You can't keep on working as you have been, Jean; your health will break down."

"I do not think it will," she answered, "but thank you for being concerned about me. I love helping my mother all I can, and things are not too hard when you do them for love's sake."

Love to the Lord is the inspiration of all our service to others, for we love Him who first loved us. Is it this love which charges our activity with delight? Many tasks are not attractive in themselves, but love enables us to do them with a song on our lips. Service done in a spirit of love is what really counts for God and helps others.[3]

Jean's compensation was not in money but in the satisfaction of doing something for her mother, and the praise of her friends and fellow workers for her unselfish services. Thinking of God's love, ought we not to serve others unselfishly?

Within the reach of everyone who reads this meditation lies the ability and the opportunity to make life more meaningful and less lonely for somebody else every day. Such occasions are like miracles and are the continual works of thoughtful hearts. Many years ago the beloved English minister John Henry Jowett wrote a short devotion called "Sixpenny-worth of Miracle." He told of a man who had come across a little boy crying as if his heart would break because he had lost sixpence which he had been given to pay a debt. The man, reporting what he had done, said: "Sixpence dropped by the wayside, and a whole family made wretched. I put my hand in my pocket and wrought sixpenny worth of miracle." A sixpence has less value than an American dime. Let your imagination loose on that. Think of going through the world performing ten-cent miracles.

Behind the simple deed of a stranger soothing a child's

---

[3] Gordon Chilvers, *The Upper Room*, May 21, 1965.

anxieties by replacing a lost coin is an exciting truth. God has entrusted few of us with the capacity to do great deeds which may change the face of the world. But to none of us has he denied the rewarding work of the ten-cent miracle. Are we too preoccupied with our own cares to see the need of some simple ministry to human need? Or do we shun the little "miracles" because we are waiting around for a great spectacular one?

No one ever had a more thoughtful, kind, considerate, patient, and lovable companion than I am blessed with. As I write this meditation, she has gone for a brief visit with a former neighbor, a lovable Jewish friend, ninety years old. When she leaves there, she will take this lovely person across town to spend the evening with her older brother, who lives alone except for a maid who comes during the day. Hundreds of times I have heard my wife say: "It is not always that you have an opportunity to do a kindness for someone, and I always get an inner satisfaction in doing what I can." Gratitude on the part of the recipient of these deeds of kindness is one of life's compensations for her.

In Matthew 25 Jesus describes the division between the righteous and the evil ones at the last judgment. He says that the basis for the determination of one's destiny will be the response he has given to human need. Life's compensations will be meted out at such a time.

Imagine a sea of faces, each singled out as if he stood alone before divine judgment, being asked not about his creed or his denomination or his reputation, but about his relationship with people in the little unconscious, unremembered acts of life. "Inasmuch as ye have [or have not] done it unto one of the least of these my brethren, ye have [or have not] done it unto me." The test will be unerring; the compensations will be surprising and in many instances,

shocking. There are two destinies—life and death. The crite-
rion will be whether or not we have given help or done some
kindness when the opportunities came.

There are many areas in the history of Christianity in
which life's compensations have been rewarding, but medical missions has always had its heroes, its martyrs, its unselfish servants. For Southern Baptists, the story of Bill Wallace
of China, has been the inspiration of unnumbered volunteers
for missionary work for the past thirty years.

Go with me in your imagination to a garage in the back-
yard of a physician's home in Knoxville, Tennessee. The
date—July 5, 1925.

There was almost no breeze. In the stillness it seemed time was
suspended, as indeed it was for Bill Wallace. Inside the garage
where he sat, the shadows offered some relief from the brilliant
sunshine which reached in from the opened doors to expose a
partially dismantled Ford, a grimy but orderly workbench, an
assortment of oil-smeared wrenches, and a small New Testament
open on the bench.

The physician's seventeen-year-old son, whose main claim to
fame was his phenomenal mechanical skill, was working dili-
gently when his moment of destiny seized him. The first assault
slowed him; the second caused a mistake; the third stopped him.

Laying aside his wrench, he picked up his New Testament as
if it could offer an answer to the demanding question that
without warning had taken command of his consciousness. What
should he do with his life? No, that was not quite so accurate. He
was not sure the question was so self-determinative. Better, what
would God have him do with his life?

An intruder . . . would not have realized that forces at work in
this young man on this hot, still, uninspiring afternoon would
forever decide his life's course. Neither the place, . . . not even
the slouching figure of the lean, sandy-haired youth, would
have revealed it; but that is what was happening. . . . Can God's

Holy Spirit grasp men and set them apart for special tasks in such ordinary circumstances? Well, it was, and he did; and it happened right there in the garage.[4]

Nine years later, Bill Wallace had completed his medical education, served his internship, and was resident in surgery in Knoxville's General Hospital. He knew God had called him as a medical missionary, but where, he did not know. In faraway Wuchow, one of China's ancient cities, Dr. Robert E. Beddoe of Stout Memorial Hospital was pouring out his heart, seeking through the Foreign Mission Board, Richmond, Virginia, their help in securing a much-needed surgeon. Bill Wallace was to be the answer to their call.

September 6, 1935, he sailed from San Francisco to begin nearly seventeen years of unselfish, sacrificial service in ministering to the thousands of China's lost, unsaved, disease-ridden people. He became a legend among the people he served, but at the peak of his ministry, he was called upon to seal his Christian witness with his life, a martyr for Christ in a Communist prison cell. He could have remained in Knoxville to be associated with an eminent physician and earned financial security, but Bill Wallace's compensation as a dedicated servant of God was to say with Paul: "For to me to live is Christ, and to die is gain" (Phil. 1:21). At his grave, on a simple shaft reaching heavenward, these words are engraved.

Life's greatest compensation will be, in the words of Matthew 25:21, "Well done, thou good and faithful servant: thou hast been faithful over a few things, I will make thee ruler over many things: enter thou into the joy of thy lord."

---

[4] Jesse C. Fletcher, *Bill Wallace of China* (Nashville: Broadman Press, 1963), p. 3.

10
No Man Is an Island

In nearly all phases of athletics, "teamwork" accounts for the success of the event and is an inspiration to the spectators. For years the New York Yankees dominated the professional baseball world. Year after year they were champions of the American League and went on to win the World Series. The 1963 series was a different story. The Los Angeles Dodgers accomplished an almost unheard-of victory by defeating the Yankees in four straight games. The hero of the series was pitcher Sandy Koufax. In the opening game he stopped "murderers row" in their tracks, winding up the game by striking out his sixteenth batter, a new World Series record.

Koufax was on an island, the pitcher's mound in the middle of the diamond, but he never could have led his team to two of the victories without the magnificent support of his teammates. He could not do it alone. No man is an island. No man stands alone. Every individual needs encouragement and the moral support of another. As Paul wrote to the Romans: "None of us liveth to himself, and no man dieth to himself. For whether we live, we live unto the Lord; and whether we die, we die unto the Lord: whether we live therefore, or die, we are the Lord's. For to this end Christ both died, and rose, and revived, that he might be Lord both of the dead and living" (14:7–9).

Through all the centuries of recorded time, men have set in motion influences that affect my life and your life today. We are all the heirs of the ages. Men reaching for the stars have created for you, and for me, a world of wonder and challenge. As citizens of this great country which we proudly call America, there are living in me and in you the ideals of the ragged soldiers of Valley Forge, the gallant pilgrims, the daring explorers and pioneers, the fighters for freedom through all of our history.

Nearly 350 years ago, John Donne gave to the reading public a group of devotions, one of which has inspired the challenge I hope to leave with you in this message. Devotions XVII is a challenge which will make us conscious of our responsibility to try and render some little service to help make our world a better place in which to live—a world of brotherhood and goodwill for all people.

No man is an island, entire of itself; every man is a piece of the continent, a part of the main; if a clod is washed away by the sea, Europe is the less, as well as if a promontory were, as well as if a manor of thy friends or of thine own were; any man's death diminishes me, because I am involved in mankind; and therefore never send to know for whom the bell tolls; it tolls for thee.

Three hundred years later two musicians, using the thoughts expressed by this godly man, composed a song and made it into a choral arrangement for Fred Waring and his Pennsylvanians:

> No man is an island,
> No man stands alone.

Each man's joy is joy to me,
Each man's grief is my own.
We need one another,
So I will defend,
Each man as my brother,
Each man as my friend.

I saw the people gather,
I heard the music start;
The song that they were singing
Is ringing in my heart.[1]

Too many of us fail to realize that we are recipients of untold blessings from those who have gone before. Sydney J. Harris, in one of his syndicated articles appearing in hundreds of newspapers, made some striking observations about one of the many school dropouts in our high schools. The lad's teachers had warned him that unless he changed his ways, he was sure to flunk his work. They tried to impress upon him his debt to his parents, his community, and to the past. His answer was, "What do I care about the past? I just want to live in the present. I want to get out with my hot rod."

"The boy is not a failure," said Harris, "his education is. His education at home as well as at school. His education in feelings as well as in subjects. He lacks the first requisite of a civilized human being: respect and gratitude for the past." Like Robinson Crusoe, he failed to realize that he is not alone in this world. He is dependent on others in many ways.

He loves his hot rod, but he does not understand it—and nothing is truer than that we cannot truly love or possess what

---

[1] *No Man Is an Island.* Words and arrangement by Roy Ringlan, Joan Whitney, and Alexander Kramer. Distributed by Shawnee Press, Inc., Delaware Water Gap, Penn. Used by permission.

we do not understand. He is doomed to a life of brief sensations and deep disappointments. . . .

He could work a lifetime and never invent one element of the modern motorcar. He gives no thought to the men of the past who labored to make his hot rod possible. To the men who worked long hours, often for little or no pay, to advance man's knowledge a step further. To the men who lived for the future, who handed this legacy down to him.

Everything he has—and never thinks about—is inherited from men better than he. His clothes (who invented the loom?), his shoes (who learned to tan leather?), his jazz records (who captured the sound on a plate and reproduced it through a machine?). . . .

He himself is a beggar, an object of charity, a pathetic creature who left alone could not devise an alphabet, conceive a wheel, put electricity to use, solve a single geometrical problem that brought the Pyramids to the newest skyscraper whose penthouse he so covets.

Independent? Free? Living in the present? Without the accumulated store of the past, he could not survive a week by his own intelligence. If all others, in past centuries, had been like him, not a single part of the life he thinks he enjoys today would be here.

The boy and his hot rod. What a tragedy, what a loss, what an ironic reversal of values, that the piece of machinery is such a stunning success, and the human being who "owns" it is so inferior to his possession.

Yes, what a tragedy! He lived as though "he lived alone," wholly unconscious of his debt to others. At the same time, and on a more personal note, his mother, father, teachers, church and pastor, and intimate friends failed him. More enduring than skyscrapers, bridges, cathedrals, and other material symbols of man's achievements are the invisible monuments of wisdom, inspiration, and example erected in

the hearts of men. Example has immortal momentum. It has
been truly said that a boy does not have to be shown a mark
on the wall to measure up to when there is a man around the
size he wants to be.

One day in the last century [a] young lad sat in the gallery of
the British House of Commons and listened to the majestic
eloquence of John Bright. He went back home with the resolve
in his heart that he was going to be a lawyer. The day before he
was to sign the articles in a law office, he was walking through
his native city when he came face to face with his Sunday school
teacher. He said: "I am signing the articles in a law office
tomorrow." The Sunday school teacher said, "That is a great
profession," and then his face clouded and he continued, "but
Henry, I have always hoped that you would be a minister of
Christ." In deep thought the youth went home and there in
solitude he heard the call of the Eternal ringing in the chambers
of his soul, "as clearly as the morning bell rings in the valleys of
Switzerland" and John Henry Jowett entered the Christian ministry. In Great Britain and in America he exercised a ministry
second to none in the twentieth century.[2]

Going his own way, as one man on an island, John Henry
Jowett might have failed as a lawyer; but had that Sunday
School teacher failed in his responsibility, the Christian
church would have lost a consecrated minister. "I think of
the day that humble Sunday school teacher stood in the
presence of his Master and in glad surprise heard him say,
'Well done, thou good and faithful servant: enter thou into
the joy of thy lord.' And John Henry Jowett didn't hear any
greater praise when he stood in the presence of the King of
kings." Enduring and abiding was the satisfaction of an

    [2] John Sutherland Bonnell, *What Are You Living For?* (Nashville:
Abingdon Press, 1950), p. 155.

unknown servant of our Lord who did what he could to influence another life. The people of the past are represented in the people of the present.

Spring practice for the Vanderbilt University football team came to a close, April 30, 1964. An intersquad game was played on the evening of May 1. At half time during the intermission, Coach Jack Green presented to an "unknown" scrub player, Tom Crawford, a lineman of Vanderbilt's 1963 B team, a plaque in recognition of service "beyond the call of duty."

Crawford transferred to Vanderbilt from Cornell University where he had been studying chemical engineering. He came without an athletic scholarship. He had changed his major and Vanderbilt was his choice of schools. Being a senior in the 1963–64 class he was under no obligation to participate in spring practice. But, said one of the assistant coaches, "He never shied away from contact when he might have. He always jumped right in wherever we needed a volunteer. He's played guard, tackle, or end. The guy seemed to enjoy getting banged around. He must have known we were not considering him for the varsity in 1963, but it didn't dampen his enthusiasm. He never stopped giving everything he had."

In making the presentation, Coach Green said, "Tom Crawford typifies the loyal, conscientious scrub who loves football and has given his all to help make the team a success. He had very little hope of ever playing on the varsity, but he wanted to be a part of our team. He came out and devoted his time to our cause. He made a definite contribution. This plaque goes to him with our genuine appreciation."

Tom Crawford was fully conscious that "no man is an island. No man stands alone. Each man is my brother. We need one another." Unselfishly, he made his contribution that Vanderbilt might have a winning team, even after his graduation.

There are so many avenues of service, of usefulness, of unselfish giving of oneself to help make our world a better place in which to live. The radiant words of the Sermon on the Mount light the spirits of each generation. The axioms of the great inspire men to "rise on stepping-stones of their dead selves to higher things." Simple words expressing courage, faith, and love have immortal significance in the lives of millions. As you throw the weight of your influence on the side of the good, the true, and the beautiful, your life will achieve an endless splendor—an "abiding satisfaction" that what you may have done or said will go on in others, making them bigger, finer, nobler than you ever dared to hope. You are not an island; you are part of the whole.

To be the greatest blessing, the greatest influence for good, your life must be linked with Jesus'. After Peter and John had healed the lame man in the Temple in Jerusalem, they were questioned by the rulers, elders, and scribes as to their authority. Then followed one of Peter's great sermons, as recorded in Acts 4. "Now when they [the rulers, elders, and scribes] saw the boldness of Peter and John, and perceived that they were unlearned and ignorant men, they marvelled; and they took knowledge of them, that they had been with Jesus" (v. 13).

As you witness for Christ, help men to grow in Christlikeness, and work for peace, understanding, and good will, your influence will merge with the good influence of men of every age into the eternal stream of God's goodness.

11
Somewhere, Someone Prayed

The weary one had rest, the sad one had joy that day,
    And wondered how.
A ploughman singing at his work had prayed,
    "Lord, help them now."
Away in foreign lands they wondered how
    Their feeble words had power.
At home the Christians, two or three, had met
    To pray an hour.
Yes, we are always wondering, wondering how,
    Because we do not see
Someone, unknown perhaps, and far away,
    On bended knee.

The phrase "Prayer changes things" has been a much-used expression by Christians for hundreds of years, and there are scores of God's children who will bear witness to the fact. We have seen it painted on posters which adorn the walls of our Sunday School rooms; we have read it in the Bible, heard it from the pulpit, and seen answers to prayers among our friends. Driving through Knoxville, Tennessee, we saw a sign on a church bulletin board, "No day is well spent without a talk with God."

Several years ago a survey was made of a number of congregations in the area of New York City as to the kind of sermon they would like to hear preached or the topics they would like to hear discussed from the pulpit. It was most interesting to observe the wide range of answers. Some were rather strange, but predominantly they were earnest and sincere, giving evidence of help needed in the lives of many individuals. The topic which had the majority of votes concerned prayer, or how to pray.

This, of course, is not a new question. It was asked by the disciples of Jesus, whom we acknowledge to be the Master of the art of prayer. Even though the disciples came from varied backgrounds, we have to believe that they had been brought up as devout Hebrews. We would hope that they were accustomed to family prayers. As they worshiped in the synagogue on the sabbath day, they joined in public prayers. But in their close association with Jesus, they found that he manifested a prayer life that was beyond their comprehension. It was entirely different from the memorized prayers used in the synagogue.

When Jesus knelt in prayer, he prayed with such earnestness, such joy, that his countenance was transformed. His disciples had never heard prayers uttered with such fervor. Marveling at his prayer life, is it any wonder that they pleaded with him, "Lord, teach us to pray?" Then followed the "prayer pattern" he would have us use, known throughout the centuries as "The Lord's Prayer." We will use in another chapter an application of this prayer to our daily life, taken from a meditation by William Russell Bowie. But first let us look at two dramatic situations in the Gospels which clearly showed results when "somewhere, someone prayed."

The Roman ruler of Judea, Herod Agrippa, decided to

stamp out the dedicated followers of the crucified Galilean
by throwing their leader, Peter, into prison.

Now about that time Herod the king stretched forth his hands
to vex certain of the church. And he killed James the brother of
John with the sword. And because he saw it pleased the Jews, he
proceeded further to take Peter also. (Then were the days of
unleavened bread.) And when he had apprehended him, he put
him in prison, and delivered him to four quaternions of soldiers
to keep him; intending after Easter to bring him forth to the
people. Peter therefore was kept in prison: but prayer was made
without ceasing of the church unto God for him (Acts 12:1-5).

Peter was securely guarded, or so thought Herod. Sixteen
soldiers had charge of this important prisoner. Two of them
were chained to him, one on either side. Other guards
watched at the inner and outer doors. Peter was safely se-
cured. He had no chance of escape.

But no! Somewhere, someone prayed. In a house in the
city, in the home of Mary, the mother of John Mark, Peter's
brethren were gathered, and prayer for his release and
safety was being offered. For a week they had been praying.
Praying in earnest—praying with passionate conviction that
God's servant would be released, that somehow the Lord
would intervene in Peter's behalf. He was their leader and
the cause of Christ would be hindered without him and his
passionate zeal to preach God's message to the lost.

Things began to happen at the prison. Gates, chains, and
guards could keep out visitors and keep in prisoners, but
they could not keep out our Lord's angels, messengers of
deliverance and mercy.

Behold, the angel of the Lord came upon him, and a light
shined in the prison: and he smote Peter on the side, and raised

him up, saying, Arise up quickly. And his chains fell off from his hands. And the angel said unto him, Gird thyself, and bind on thy sandals. And so he did. And he saith unto him, Cast thy garment about thee, and follow me (vv. 7–9).

Led by the angel, Peter followed as one in a dream. The cool night air outside the prison brought him the realization that he was a free man. Following the leading of the angel, he came to the house which served as headquarters of his brethren—yes, the meeting place, an unknown place where someone had been praying.

Read the rest of this dramatic deliverance of one of God's own. Even his own brethren could hardly believe what their eyes saw. But had not our Saviour taught for years, "If ye abide in me, and my words abide in you, ye shall ask what ye will, and it shall be done unto you" (John 15:7)? For nearly two thousand years Christ's words have challenged men to follow his patterns for life's days, to be bold for him, to do great and audacious works in his name. But too often we do not accept his patterns, not only in our prayer life, but in the great decisions of life. We repeat again, "No day is well spent without a talk with God." Just as prayer "changed things" for Peter, so it will for us.

The story of Paul and Silas and the Philippian jailer is another demonstration of the power of prayer. In this instance it was the men themselves who poured out their hearts to God. Yet we must believe their friends who, after hearing of their imprisonment, likewise were praying for them. Their story is a familiar one. For several weeks they had been telling the story of salvation to an unbelieving people. They had found Lydia, a seller of purple, who worshiped their God, and she was baptized, and her household. Encouraged, they continued their ministry until they ran into trouble with wicked men who were using a certain damsel for their own selfish interests. On the basis of their complaint these noble servants were beaten and thrown into prison. Then the miracle happened. At midnight they prayed and sang praises unto God. We know the results. The foundations of the prison were shaken, the doors were opened, and everyone's bands were loosed. In desperation the keeper of the prison would have killed himself. "But Paul cried with a loud voice, saying, Do thyself no harm: for we are all here" (16:28). Then followed the conversion of the jailer and his household. Were you to ask Paul how all these things happened he would humbly answer, "We prayed." During the Reformation and the days of Martin Luther, he said, "All who call upon God in true faith, earnestly from the heart, will certainly be heard, and will receive what they have asked and desired."

"What is prayer?" A woman once wrote this question on a little deaf and dumb girl's slate.

"Prayer is the wish of the heart," the little girl wrote with her chalk. This is the promise of the Scriptures: We can ask anything that is the will of the Father, any wish that we hold in our heart. God will always answer prayer. Sometimes God says yes and sometimes he says no. Quiet, humble prayer, practiced with diligence and sincere faith, will turn your life into a deep, rich, exhilarating experience. In our hearts prayer creates serenity, strength, and light in the most extraordinary way. From an inner depth one has not known, unbelievable things can happen.

Many stories of faith, courage, and physical endurance came out of World War II, but few can demonstrate the power of prayer as does the one about Captain Eddie Rickenbacker and the group of men with him who drifted for twenty-one days in the wide expanse of the Pacific Ocean.

Their plane, on a war mission, had been forced down at sea. Launching the three emergency life rafts, tied together with ropes, they had drifted for eight days in the scorching tropic sun. Their feet were blistered, their faces burned, their mouths and bodies parched. Four small oranges had been their only food. The heat, the hunger, the exhaustion had brought them close to the breaking point.

Eddie Rickenbacker believed in prayer. He had learned it as a child at his mother's knee, and in many crises of his life, prayer had given him comfort and courage. All of his companions were young men, facing their first great trial. They could not have been called religious, yet one of them produced a small Bible from his jacket pocket. It had been issued as a matter of routine, but it was to prove a guiding light in this time of extreme emergency. Perhaps at the suggestion of Captain Eddie, they took turns reading it aloud every day, both morning and evening, following up with a period of prayer.

On the eighth day of their hunger and thirst, the noble little band of men were desperate. There had been no sign of a rescue plane or ship. At the customary time on that day one of the men read from the sixth chapter of Matthew where our Saviour was urging trust in the Father's care as a cure for worry and anxiety.

Jesus said:

Therefore I say unto you, Take no thought for your life, what ye shall eat, or what ye shall drink; nor yet for your body, what ye shall put on. Is not the life more than meat, and the body more than raiment? (v. 25).

Your heavenly Father knoweth that ye have need of all these things. But seek ye first the kingdom of God, and his righteousness; and all these things shall be added unto you (vv. 32–33).

As if by a miracle a semblance of relief came to these suffering men. A sea gull flew out from nowhere and landed on Rickenbacker's head. Cautiously he reached up and caught it, and they had their first food. Every edible part was consumed, including the small bones. The innards were saved and used for fishing bait. Again they had food after catching several small fish. Soon thereafter they ran into a rainstorm, and they had fresh water for drinking. Their prayers had been answered. This new experience filled the men with awe and astonishment. From then on they prayed with renewed confidence. Captain Eddie assured them that God was with them and that they would be saved.

For two weeks longer they drifted, weak, emaciated, and more nearly dead than alive. At last on the twenty-first day they were spotted by searching planes and picked up. It was a miraculous rescue. When the news of the rescue was flashed around the world, people everywhere were excited. People who had not prayed for years began to do so again. Some who had never prayed in their lives began to search their souls with renewed faith and courage.

As soon as the brave little group had recovered enough for an interview, Rickenbacker expressed the gratitude of his associates and then humbly said, "We prayed." He was aware of the fact that all over the world, friends and fellow servicemen had been praying for their rescue.

Gordon Cooper, America's twenty-two-orbit hero, rode through a din down Pennsylvania Avenue in Washington, but he was an even greater hero to Christians all over the land, when amid a hush, he read to the assembled Congress a simple prayer he brought down from the sky. Legislators, Supreme Court justices, and diplomats bowed their heads as he read the prayer composed while in flight: "Be with our families. Give them guidance and encouragement and let them know that everything will be OK." In the presidential gallery Mrs. Hattie Cooper, the astronaut's mother, covered her eyes with a hand, then brushed away the tears and smiled. She was conscious of the fact that all during his flight, somewhere, thousands were praying for her son.

We all owe our gratitude to unknown Christians who still believe that God answers prayer.

The Japanese can dwarf trees. They can take a cherry or maple tree and dwarf it so it will never grow taller than 12 or 18 inches. They cut out the taproot and the tree lives only by its surface roots.

It lives, but it cannot grow. Leave prayer out of the lives of children in our grammar schools, high schools, and colleges, and you have taken away a vital force in their lives. They may grow intellectually, but you cut out the taproot of their spiritual life. We repeat, "No day is well spent without a talk with God."

In the closing hours of our Saviour's life, as he talked with the disciples in the passover chamber, he said: "Whatsoever ye shall ask in my name, that will I do, that the Father may be glorified" (John 14:13). A promise, and a privilege of prayer. May we join individuals and groups who, somewhere, are pleading that our patterns of life may be Christlike.

12
Integrity, A Priceless Virtue

It was a beautiful, warm, spring morning in Nashville, Tennessee, May, 1963. Folding three twenty-dollar bills and placing them in his shirt pocket, C. C. (Kit) Carson, a staff barber at the Hermitage Hotel, made his way leisurely down Union Street to the American National Bank to get some change for the day's operations. Upon arrival at the teller's window he discovered that the money was missing, having slipped through a hole in his shirt pocket.

Red-faced and embarrassed, he returned to the shop and reported the loss to his employer. Someone suggested a "Want Ad" in the lost-and-found column of the afternoon paper.

The shop had hardly opened the next morning when the messenger from the Baptist Sunday School Board, Henry Lee Kage, walked in and asked for Mr. Carson. Handing the three twenties, still folded, to Carson, he said, "I found these on Union Street and saw your ad in the paper."

"Is there anything I can do for you?" inquired Carson.

Kage only said, "Anything you want to give me will be all right."

"Here's your reward," said Mr. Carson, as he handed Kage thirty dollars.

Kage's self-respect was more important to him than sixty dollars found on the street, and his integrity did not go unrewarded.

Sixty dollars seems like pocket change compared to the $240,000 found in a canvas bag on the streets of Los Angeles by the Douglas Johnsons in March, 1961. But the same principle of honesty is involved. The bag, stamped "Federal Reserve Bank," had been dropped accidentally from the rear door of a Brink's armored truck as the money was being transported to the bank's headquarters. Realizing that the money did not belong to them, the Johnsons immediately notified the FBI, who went to their home, collected the money, and returned it to its rightful owners. A reward of $10,000 was paid the Johnsons.

For the next several weeks from all over the country came words of praise and commendation for their integrity in returning the money. Mail had to be delivered in bundles. On a Los Angeles postcard was scribbled: "I'm glad there is at least one honest man around." From a mother came the message, "You did a great service in pricking the conscience of a great many people. Knowing there are people like you around makes me feel more hopeful about this world. Thanks for living. I'm glad you were born." Yes, honesty and integrity are priceless virtues.

Still another example, on a much smaller scale, was demonstrated by a ten-year-old girl, Barbara Cannon, of Memphis, Tennessee. Barbara was at church on Sunday night. After the services she went to a pay telephone and called her parents to tell them that she had a ride home with a relative. When she hung up the phone, eighty cents fell into the coin return slot. Arriving at home she told her parents what had happened and her father asked her what she thought she should do about it. Without hesitation the girl said it should be returned to the telephone company. And this she did the next day, with a note explaining what had happened. The divisional commercial manager said it was the first time in ten years that such a thing had happened in Memphis. He sent Barbara a nice letter with a gift—a charm bracelet.

It was the honest and honorable thing to do, wrote the manager. Where had this child learned the pattern of honesty? In the home, of course, and great is the responsibility of parents for teaching this cherished virtue.

In contrast to these three examples, let us look at the other side of the picture. The following story, which originally appeared in *Guideposts* magazine, was printed one morning in Rabbi Jerome Kestenbaum's devotional column in the *Nashville Tennessean*.

When Jimmy was six years old he was with his father when they were caught speeding. His father handed the officer a five-dollar bill along with his driver's license. "It's OK, Son," his father said when they drove off. "Everybody does it."

When he was twelve, he broke his glasses on the way to school. His mother persuaded the insurance company that they had been stolen and they collected $32.00. "It's OK, Son," she said. "Everybody does it."

When Jimmy was nineteen he was approached by a classmate in college who offered the test answers for five dollars. "It's OK, Kid," he said. "Everybody does it."

Jimmy was caught and sent home in disgrace. "How could you do this to me and your mother?" his father said. "You never learned anything like this at home."

The writer of the original article made a further observation. "If there is one thing parents can't stand it is a kid who cheats. What our children need are models—not critics!"

The rise of cheating among high school and college students is appalling and is causing great concern to educators. Schools that once boasted of "honor systems," under which teachers wrote the exam on the blackboard and then left the room, are now having second thoughts. The cheater knocks off splendid grades. Disgusted fellow students hesitate to report him because Americans have been more tolerant of the horse thief than of the stool pigeon.

There is general agreement that much of the rise in cheating is the pressure to meet certain standards—pressure to pass the college boards, pressure to produce a transcript high enough to stave off the draft boards. But there is no other way to assess the admissibility or promotability of a student than to examine the quality of his work and the depth of his knowledge.

Honesty is merely that degree to which the individual resists the temptation to take unfair advantage. The cheater does more than pass an exam. He is setting a pattern that may follow him through life. He does more than rob his competitor or enrich his own pocketbook; he can endanger us all. Who wants to be up in a plane with a pilot who cheated to get his instrument rating, and who, when an emergency arises, will be unable to read all of the instruments on the complicated instrument board? Or who wants a doctor who bought his medical exam answers from a safecracker?

Few things shocked the schools of our armed services as did the disclosure of widespread cheating among the cadets at the Air Force Academy at Colorado Springs in the spring of 1965, most of which was among the freshman class. It was impossible to determine the amount of profit made by the few ringleaders. However, 105 cadets resigned, leaving a black eye on a trusted institution of learning, and disgrace to those involved. Somewhere along life's highway, someone had set the wrong pattern. If our youngsters are talked to plainly and warned of the consequences, most of them will get the message.

I think one of the most tragic pictures I ever saw was one which came out of Miami, Florida. Seated at a table in police headquarters was Fred Harrison Haney. His middle and index fingers pointed to two pennies on the table, and the caption of the picture read: "Wages of Sin: 2 Cents." Said Haney, "This is the only remaining capital I have left from more than forty-nine years of stealing." But he wasn't bitter. "It's too late now," Haney said, as he waited for deputies to take him back to a Texas prison from which he had been released after serving part of a ninety-nine-year sentence for robbery. White-haired, his face lined and wrinkled, he made the soul-searching statement, "I'm too old to steal anymore."

Tragic, that the sunset years of a life which might have been of service to God and mankind had not been channeled into a life of usefulness.

Centuries ago God gave Moses ten rules for living. The eighth rule of life reads, "Thou shalt not steal." Jesus gave us another pattern for living known as the "Golden Rule." Both should be looked upon as the foundation of our whole economic system because they recognize the fact that every individual has a God-given right to work, to earn a living, to save, and to own something. To take away from one that which is rightfully his is wrong in the sight of God and man.

The J. C. Penney Company is well known throughout America. Its founder is a dedicated Christian and attributes much of his success to fair dealing with his customers.

When I first entered business the doctrine of *caveat emptor*—let the buyer beware—prevailed. If a man tried to operate his enterprise that way today he would soon be out of business.

Today business must be conducted by the principle of the Golden Rule. Nothing has yet come along to convince me that the Rule should be repealed.

I have never seen a time in which a man could break the rules of ethics and still be a success.

The teachings of my father, a farmer and lay Baptist preacher, guided my business principles. Long ago I decided that my business should be operated on a basis of integrity, with service and goods as represented.

I called my first store—a butcher shop—"The Golden Rule." The best and most profitable customer was the town's leading hotel. My meat cutter advised me to buy the hotel's chef a bottle of whiskey each week, as he did the hotel's meat buying. After I had done so once, a strange feeling came over me. I thought of my father and what he would have done. I determined then and there never again would I bribe the chef or anyone else to get business. I lost the trade of the hotel and because of that also lost the butcher shop and $300 I had saved penny by penny. I might have become a successful butcher. But then I would probably not have founded the J. C. Penney Company.

When I face a question of business choice, I ask myself, Is this worth my best? Besides the Golden Rule, I believe there are five other important rules for success: preparedness, hard work, honesty, confidence in men, and appeal to spirit.

I don't want to be known as a wealthy man when I pass on. I want to be known as a man who tried to accomplish some good. If I had my life to live over again and I could be more unselfish in sharing profits, I would.[1]

Shocked as we may be by the almost daily reports of scandals in high and low places, of tax officials accepting payoffs for not collecting sales taxes, and other reports of bank robberies, there are still many, many people who are

---

[1] J. C. Penney, "Viewpoint," Philadelphia *Inquirer*, November 3, 1963. Used by permission.

above reproach when it comes to their personal integrity.

Aaron Burr was perhaps a more brilliant man than George Washington. If he had been loyal to the truth, he would have been an abler man; but what made Washington the chief hero of our great republic was his sagacity, not his intellectual genius. Over and over again Washington voiced his appraisal of integrity. "I hope I shall always possess firmness and virtue enough to maintain, what I consider the most enviable of titles, the character of an 'honest man.'"

Benjamin Franklin was equally firm in his belief that honesty is a priceless virtue. "Let honesty be as the breath of thy soul; and never forget to have a penny, when all thy expenses are enumerated and paid: then shalt thou reach the point of happiness and independence shall be thy shield and buckler, thy helmet and crown; then shall thy soul walk upright nor stoop to the silken wretch because he hath riches, nor pocket an abuse because the hand which offers it wears a ring set with diamonds." As the sun has no need to boast of its brightness, nor the moon of her effulgence, honest and courageous people have very little to say either about their courage or their honesty.

The writer of Proverbs in counseling his sons cautioned them, "Keep thy heart with all diligence; for out of it are the issues of life" (4:23). The heart, in those days, was thought to include the mind as well as the emotions; it was seen as the seat of the spiritual life. Thus, the heart was the focal point of man's integrity. David prayed, "Create in me a clean heart, O God; and renew a right spirit within me" (Psalm 51:10). From the innermost recesses of a clean heart will come pure and clean thoughts. Jesus' teachings were rooted in the wisdom and counseling of the Hebrew sages and psalmists. He seems to have been setting a goal for purity in living when he said, "Blessed are the pure in heart, for they shall see God." A life of integrity can come only from the pure in heart.

All parents look with pride on their children, and wish for them the best of everything in life. An American poet, Ona Freeman Lathrop, has voiced the hope of every good mother in her poem "A Mother's Reward":

> I do not ask that you repay
> The hours of toil and pain,
> The sacrifice of youth and strength
> Shall not have been in vain.
> I do not ask gratitude
> But only this, my child,
> That you shall live your life so well
> My gifts be not defiled.
>
> The nights I watched beside your crib,
> The years of love and care
> Will amply be repaid if once
> I see you standing there—
> An upright and honest soul
> On whom success has smiled,
> That I may say with humble pride
> —"That is my child!" [2]

---

[2] *American Voices,* ed. Margaret Nelson (New York: Avon Books, 1939).

13
When Shadows Fall

Several years ago two pictures appeared on the front page of our afternoon paper. One was of a young mother with a baby in her arms and a three-year-old girl by her side. With umbrella raised, and waiting for the traffic light to change, the mother was on her way to the doctor's office. The other picture was of a United States Weather Bureau meteorologist checking the velocity of the rainy winds of a dying hurricane. Over these two pictures was this line: "Into each life some rain must fall."

Longfellow describes the trials we all must face in his poem "The Rainy Day." The closing verse of the poem offers us words of comfort and assurance for those "dark and dreary" days:

> The day is cold, and dark, and dreary;
> It rains, and the wind is never weary;
> The vine still clings to the mouldering wall,
> But at every gust the dead leaves fall,
> And the day is dark and dreary.
>
> My life is cold, and dark, and dreary;
> It rains, and the wind is never weary;

My thoughts still cling to the mouldering Past,
But the hopes of youth fall thick in the blast,
    And the days are dark and dreary.

Be still, sad heart! and cease repining;
Behind the clouds is the sun still shining;
Thy fate is the common fate of all,
Into each life some rain must fall,
    Some days must be dark and dreary.

Norwegian writer Hans Lonner tells the story (*The Upper Room*, October 14, 1961) of a man who knew how to face the storms of life.

In Sandefjord, Norway, is a gravestone with this inscription: "The Lord's ways are always good, but not always easy for a human being to travel. Let us, however, say thanks for the ways of the Lord."

Behind the writing of this unusual inscription is a tragic story, yet one that shows that God does not withhold his blessings to us in the midst of our tragedy and sorrow. One day when a traveling preacher was far from home, he received a telegram bearing tragic news. His home had burned, and his wife and two children had perished in the fire.

To some persons such a tragedy could have resulted in loss of faith, but not so for this man. On the ruins of his home where his loved ones had died, he fought a battle and won a victory. There where all his ways seemed to come to a sorrowful end, he found assurance in God's way. He found himself offering thanks to God, even in the midst of sorrow and despair.

Even if we do not understand God's purpose and ways, let us bring Him thanks at all times; for we know He loves us.

In times like these, we should say with the psalmist, "I will lift up mine eyes unto the hills, from whence cometh my help. My help cometh from the Lord, which made heaven and earth" (121:1-2).

Tragedy and sorrow slip into the life of an individual from so many avenues. When two young people come from the marriage altar and set up their home, it seems that its joy can never be disturbed—that grief can never reach their hearts. For a few years, perhaps, their fond dream remains unbroken. The flowers bloom into still softer fragrance, especially when a baby joins the family circle. Eventually there comes a day when the strange messenger of sorrow stands at the door, enters, and lays a withering hand on the precious flower of their lives.

This new experience of grief is never understood; its suddenness and strangeness add to its terribleness. What seemed an impossibility yesterday has become a reality today. It may seem that they never can be comforted, that life may never be enjoyed again. This first sorrow is to every life a most crucial moment. At no other time is wise and loving guidance so acutely needed. Friends and relatives, and one's own pastor, will rally around and offer comfort and guidance in this hour of bereavement, but an abiding faith and trust in a gracious and loving Heavenly Father can be as a shelter in times of storm. "When trouble comes, as come it must, in God a man must put his trust." Or, as the psalmist expressed it, "Then they cry unto the Lord in their trouble, and he saveth them out of their distresses" (107:19).

Death is only one of many circumstances which may cast a shadow across one's pathway. Well-made plans are frustrated, through no fault of the planner; disappointments and heartaches seem to be the lot of many; broken homes—often indirectly responsible for juvenile delinquency—or an extended illness in a home may bring sadness. All of these and many others tempt one to ask, "How is it possible to keep playing the game of life with so many ups and downs?" Again comes the answer: An abiding faith and trust in God is a never-failing source of strength and courage for each day's problems. Remember the words of the psalmist, "He restoreth my soul."

Even when shadows fall we should be grateful for the privilege of living; grateful for life with its challenges, its excitement, its rewards, and its happiness. We must come to understand that life cannot be life and have only its highlights; that living is made up of mountains and valleys, of laughter and tears, of sunshine and storm, of hope and despair. The cross of Christ shows us how we are to meet the grim side of human experience, saying to us, "Have faith in God who in a providence, the mystery of which our minds do not penetrate, uses even the crosses of the world for the world's healing."

When boarding a plane, I found myself looking into the beaming face of an old school friend. "Sit down," he said, and then added, "I don't believe we've seen each other since I lost my arm."

Three years before, his left arm had been amputated at the shoulder—bone cancer. The doctors had given him little hope. Yet, here he was, completely cured. The arm was gone, but the gay smile that I remembered from our youth was as radiant as ever; there was no trace of self-pity. He said, "My wife and I have spent the three happiest years of our lives; for when the future was uncertain, we learned to focus on the important things in life."

It is well demonstrated in botany that pruning branches strengthens the central plant. By talking with my friend, I readily saw that this pruning had not brought defeat. Rather, with God's help, he had actually grown stronger and surer of life's

richest meaning. On the mountains of life, God's help turns
stumbling blocks into toeholds.[1]

God in his wisdom has given us not only a way to ask for
the good things of earth, but a means to learn to do without
them if need be. Prayer is not a means whereby we escape
the difficult, but it is the way to become strong to meet these
emergencies. No matter how hard the way of life may become for us, or how bitter the grief we may carry in our
hearts, we should always be supremely certain that a gracious and loving Father in heaven hears us when we turn to
him in prayer.

There are rich blessings in store for us which can be
received only in times of sorrow. It would be a shortsighted
love indeed that would spare us from these heartaches unless
there were blessings in return. These burdens we ought to
carry courageously and trustingly. Whatever may happen,
God is the stronghold of our lives. Did not our Saviour
caution us, "In the world ye shall have tribulation; but be of
good cheer; I have overcome the world" (John 16:33)? And
the psalmist assures us, "Many are the afflictions of the righteous: but the Lord delivereth him out of them all (Psalm
34:19).

Some shadows fall upon our lives which are hard to understand. The story is told of the heroic soldier who was fatally
wounded in World War I just an hour before the armistice.
In cynical despair he cried aloud: "Isn't it just like God to do
a thing like this!"

Many people in less critical circumstances voice a similar
thought, implying that somehow God makes toys of his children, playing with them like puppets and then casting them

---

[1] Judson Graves Randolph, *The Upper Room*, June 20, 1965. Used
by permission.

aside when they are no longer interesting to him as people.

But may we recall the words of Thomas Carlyle: "All the good I ever got came to me in the shape of sorrow." Who, upon reflection, can say that they have not in some measure learned from the things which they have suffered?

Helen Keller, one of the most radiant personalities the world has ever known, is a living demonstration of how a fruitful life can be lived despite the seeming tragedy of birth defects. Imagine, if you can, what your day would be like if since waking you had heard no sound, seen no images, and been unable to communicate with anyone with your voice. The thought is so terrifying as to stop the imagination. One doesn't want to imagine such a lonely existence.

Could we love light if there were no darkness? Or sunshine if there were no storms? Many of the world's best things have been born of affliction. The sweetest songs ever sung on earth have been voiced in suffering. The richest blessings that we enjoy have come to us out of the fire. The good things we inherit from the past are the purchase of suffering and sacrifice. Our redemption comes from Gethsemane and Calvary. Our love for one another may be strong and true in the sunny days, but it never reaches its holiest and fullest expression until pain has touched our hearts and called out the hidden treasures stored up by our faith in God.

I have witnessed this among my associates of past years. Death took a noble husband in a tragic automobile accident. Still another was stricken with a heart attack as he boarded a plane in St. Louis for the West Coast. But out of these two tragic deaths the lonely companions have reached back into the inner reassurance of faith and trust in God and are today, radiant, active, and an inspiration to all their friends. The cross of Christ shows us how we are to meet the grim side of

human experience, saying to us, "Have faith in God, He's
still on his throne."

> When gray threads mar life's pattern
> And seem so out of line,
> Trust the Master Weaver,
> Who planned the whole design.
>
> For in Life's choicest patterns
> Some dark threads must appear
> To make the rose threads fairer,
> The gold more bright and clear.
>
> The pattern may seem intricate,
> And hard to understand,
> But trust the Master Weaver,
> And His steady guiding hand.

14
Be Ye Transformed

Some friends of ours bought a new home—not a new house but one which had been built several years ago. The former owners apparently were wedded to semidark colors in decorating the various rooms. In fact, the interior was rather dismal and unattractive. With some helpful suggestions from an interior decorator as to color schemes, the new owners have completely transformed it. With lighter shades on the walls and woodwork, draperies and carpets, one is impressed by the friendly, exhiliarating, refreshing atmosphere.

Nature offers a similar comparison. In the dead of winter the trees are bare of foliage, much of the grass has turned brown, no flowers with all their gorgeous colors are visible. Then comes spring and summer, and in the plan and pattern of God's providence all of nature is reborn. It is a glorious and welcomed season of the year.

As I write this in mid-October, summer is ended and the fall season is on our doorstep. Fall is often called the death of summer. But nothing could die in more splendor. Instead of giving up to the cold of winter, nature puts on its biggest show. It is being transformed. The hues of autumn, golden amber and rust reds, mingle with the last remnants of summer, presenting a dazzling contrast of colors which no April rainbow could rival. One is tempted to stare and stare as the bountiful scenery passes in panoramic review.

All of this is a gift from a gracious God who would have each of his children pattern their lives in keeping with his will, for life is like the contrasts just mentioned. Sin in its various forms creeps in, and a life is blighted. But in the plans and purposes of God, life can be transformed. One can never tell what the effects will be when a new person comes into one's experience. Christianity has been mainly the dropping of a new personal influence into the chemical composition of men's lives until their formulas, their patterns, their ways of life have been changed. Christ comes in. Believe me, he does change the equation, the pattern.

Christ never eliminated the sterling qualities that made Peter Peter and Paul Paul. The old impetuosity which characterized Peter and the imperturbable drive of Paul were still there when Christ got through to them, but thereafter their ways of life were completely transformed. One had to look twice to be quite sure it was the same life. The rich young ruler had the same opportunity, but alas, he was unwilling to give up his possessions and walk with the Master.

During the conference for single Adults at the Ridgecrest Baptist Assembly over the Labor Day weekend of September, 1965, two members of the faculty went shopping for a little souvenir to take home to their children. In a lovely gift shop nearby, they were attracted to some wood carvings of dogs. Picking up a carving of an old hound dog, one of the men said to the saleslady: "How does a man go about doing such delicate and beautiful work? Why, it is almost lifelike." Pointing to the old mountaineer sitting over in the corner, whittling away, she said: "I think he can tell you."

After greeting the wood-carver, they said to him: "Friend, how do you go about producing such beautiful work?"

"Mister, I take a piece of wood about this size (2 by 3 by 3) and *I cut away* all the wood that does not look like a hound dog."

Read that again! It is a parable of life, for if we are to be genuine Christians, there are many things which must be excluded or "cut away" from our lives. Life must be transformed, new patterns of daily living must be manifested. No one ever knew this more than the apostle Paul. Had he not lived a life of persecution against Christ's followers until he met the Master on the Damascus road?

Throughout Paul's writings, over and over again, he admonishes the young Christians of their obligations to bear witness to the things he has taught them. Writing to the little Christian community in Corinth, he said: "Therefore if any man be in Christ, he is a new creature: old things are passed away [cut away]; behold, all things are become new" (2 Cor. 5:17).

Writing to his friends in Colossae, urging them to live a new life by the power of the risen Christ, he said:

But now, put all these things behind you. No more evil temper or furious rage: no more evil thoughts or words about others, no more evil thoughts or words about God, and no more filthy conversation. Don't tell one another lies any more, for you have finished with the old man and all he did and have begun life as the new man, who is out to learn what he ought to be, according to the plan of God. In this new man of God's design there is no distinction between Greek and Hebrew, Jew or gentile, foreigner or savage, slave or free men. Christ is all that matters, for Christ lives in them all. As, therefore, God's picked representatives of the new humanity, purified and beloved of God himself, be merciful in action, kindly in heart, humble in mind. Accept life,

and be most patient and tolerant with one another, always ready
to forgive if you have a difference with anyone. Forgive as freely
as the Lord has forgiven you. And, above everything else, be
truly loving, for love is the golden chain of all the virtues. . . .
Let Christ's teaching live in your hearts, making you rich in the
true wisdom. Teach and help one another along the right road
with your psalms and hymns and Christian songs, singing God's
praises with joyful hearts. And whatever work you may have to
do, do everything in the name of the Lord Jesus, thanking God
the Father through him (Col. 3:5–17, Phillips).[1]

Is there any place in the Scriptures where one can find
more beautiful suggestions for a new Christian, even for all
Christians? These are glorious patterns for Christian living,
models for an individual transformed by the power of
Christ's teachings. Old habits must be discarded, unworthy
friends must be left out lest they lead one astray. As the old
wood-carver would say, "I cut away everything in life that is
not pleasing to Christ."

This is what Christ was trying to impress on Nicodemus in
the interview about the new birth. It all goes back to the
age-old question, "Can human nature be changed?" Are we
not patterned by habits developed from childhood, so that
we are what we are because of these habits, and it is often
difficult to change the character which has become a part of
our daily living?

A newspaper columnist made this observation: "If a man
is a philanderer, he will be a philanderer to the end of his
days. It is only in novels that a miracle occurs in the last chapter, that makes an alcoholic reform and become sober, the
grouch sunny and sweet-tempered, the miser generous and

---

[1] From *The New Testament in Modern English*, © J. B. Phillips,
1958. Used with permission of The Macmillan Company.

openhearted. No, in real life these things never happen. People continue to be what habit and usage made them."

If you think that this columnist is right, then you are subscribing to a very dreary and pessimistic philosophy of life. The Christian viewpoint is entirely different, for we believe that men and women can be changed, can be transformed, that there is such a thing as the new birth. Paul knew this to be true from his own experience, and he never let an opportunity pass without voicing his firm belief in the transforming power of Christ. The twelfth chapter of Romans is perhaps his most beautiful and outspoken conviction of a "pattern" for Christian living through the transforming power of Christ. At the same time it is a plea from a heart dominated by the realization of God's blessings to him.

The twelfth chapter begins with the word "Therefore," an indication that events which have taken place in the lives of Paul's beloved friends in Rome have prompted the message which he is sending in this part of his letter. In the first eight chapters the apostle is voicing his interpretation of the great doctrines of the gospel of Christ: All of his friends, both Jews and gentiles have been guilty of sin (3:9) but they have been redeemed by the grace of God and by faith in Christ Jesus and are to walk in "newness of life" (6:4). In chapters 9 to 11 Paul deals especially with his own people, the Jews, pleading for their salvation, for a new way of life. They, too, must come to God by faith in Christ. There is already a remnant of the Jews who have believed (11:5), but it is for all his fellowmen that he is outlining a transformed life, a new pattern for living.

The King James Version of this beautiful chapter is a very familiar one, yet the Phillips translation points up so many areas of life in which new patterns are needed that I have chosen to quote freely from it:

With eyes wide open to the mercies of God, I beg you, my brothers, as an act of intelligent worship, to give him your bodies as a living sacrifice, consecrated to him and acceptable by him. *Don't let the world around you squeeze you into its own mold* [its own pattern], but let God remold your minds from within, so that you may prove in practice that the plan of God for you is good, meets all his demands and moves toward the goal of true maturity.

As your spiritual teacher I give this piece of advice to each one of you. Don't cherish exaggerated ideas of yourself or your importance, but try to have a sane estimate of your capabilities by the light of the faith that God has given to you all. For just as you have many members in one physical body and those members differ in their functions, so we, though many in number, compose one body in Christ and are all members of one another (Rom. 12:1-5, Phillips).

Paul, in the succeeding verses, outlines even more patterns for Christian behavior:

Let us have *no imitation* Christian love. Let us have a genuine break with evil and a real devotion to good. Let us have *real warm affection* for one another as between brothers, and a willingness to let the other man have the credit. Let us *not allow slackness* to spoil our work and let us keep the fires of the spirit burning, as we do our work for the Lord. *Base your happiness* on your hope in Christ. When trials come endure them patiently; steadfastly maintain the habit of prayer. *Give freely* to fellow Christians in want, never grudging a meal or a bed to those who need them. And as for those who try to make your life a misery, *bless them.* Don't curse, bless. *Share the happiness* of those who are happy, and the sorrow of those who are sad. *Live in harmony with one another.* Don't become snobbish but take a real interest in ordinary people. Don't become set in your own opinions. *Don't pay back a bad turn by a bad turn, to anyone.* See that

your public behavior is above criticism. As far as your responsibility goes, *live at peace* with everyone. *Never take vengeance*
into your own hands, my dear friends: stand back and let God
punish if he will. For it is written:

Vengeance belongeth unto me: I will recompense.

And these are God's words:

If thine enemy hunger, *feed him;*

If he thirst, *give him to drink:*

For in so doing thou shalt heap coals of fire upon his head.

Don't allow yourself to be overpowered with evil.

Take the offensive—*overpower evil with good!* (vv. 9–21, author's italics).

To live this transformed life as Jesus lived, as Paul lived,
as many of our martyred missionaries have lived, means a
revolution in man's life. The Christian world has always
believed that in Jesus we learn what God is like. His ways of
graciousness have made that conviction inescapable.

But seemingly we have often overlooked the equally important fact that in Jesus we learn what we may become. We
have in him not only a revelation of divine reality but also a
view of human personality. Not only do we see in him the
divine attributes of God brought down into humanity and
these attributes demonstrated by his followers. Not only do
we see in him the splendor of God but we also see the
possibilities of human nature being transformed.

This means that we have a sizable task on our hands if we
live up to the goodness and compassion of redeemed Christians, as well as deserve the respect of our fellowmen.

If it takes Jesus to show what a man may become, it also
takes Jesus to help him become that man, and it may mean a
revolution for every professed follower of Christ if we live as
Jesus lived. We can never succeed by our devotion to
man-made principles, codes, standards, patterns, or ideals.

We must have his power in us. Did not our Saviour say: "As the branch cannot bear fruit of itself, except it abide in the vine; no more can ye, except ye abide in me. I am the vine, ye are the branches: He that abideth in me, and I in him, the same bringeth forth much fruit: for without me ye can do nothing" (John 15:4–5)?

May we ever seek to abide in Christ, that we may know his love and find our lives transformed into instruments of service for him. The miracle of Christ's love in us expresses itself in kindly words and good deeds to others.

15
Patterns of Gratitude

Each November a day of national Thanksgiving is set apart by Presidential proclamation, a day on which people in all walks of life should not fail to humble themselves before God and thank him for the blessings they have. But why wait for this particular day or season to express gratitude for untold blessings? Some 350 years ago, George Herbert, an English poet, wrote a brief prayer which could well be the prayer of everyone:

> Thou that hast given so much to me,
> Give me one thing more—a grateful heart;
> Not thankful when it pleaseth me,
> As if Thy blessings had spare days;
> But such a heart, whose pulse may be
> Thy praise.

And William Shakespeare, in *King Henry VI* expresses a similar thought:

> Poor soul! God's goodness hath been great to thee:
> Let never day nor night unhallowed pass,
> But still remember what the Lord hath done.

Gratitude is one of the most priceless habits one can cultivate, one of life's greatest virtues. Godliness, or being a Christian, is impossible without gratitude. Thankfulness is directly related to salvation, to worship, to generosity, to contentment, to personal happiness, to a happy home, to a successful business, to a life dedication. Is there any area of life in which God's goodness to his children has not been manifested?

The Bible is filled with patterns of gratitude. Read again the story of David and Jonathan, of Ruth and Naomi, of the brothers of Joseph after he had forgiven them for the tragedy of his youth when he was sold into slavery. And there are the stories of the two Marys—Mary of Bethany and Mary of Magdala.

In language so simple that a little child can understand it three of the Gospel writers have preserved for us the story of one of the most grateful souls in all literature. Jesus had journeyed to Bethany, a little village he visited often. He was a guest for the evening meal with Simon the leper. "As he sat at meat, there came a woman having an alabaster box of ointment of spikenard . . . ; and she brake the box, and poured it on his head" (Mark 14:3). The events which followed are familiar to all of us. Some of those present were incensed at what they considered a waste of something very valuable. But Jesus was conscious of the love and unselfishness which prompted this act of devotion and gratitude on the' part of Mary. Answering the astonished group, he said, "Verily I say unto you, Wheresoever this gospel shall be preached throughout the whole world, this also that she hath done shall be spoken of for a memorial of her" (Mark 14:9).

There are so many lessons for us in this simple story. Her act was an expression of the tenderest, most humble, most reverent and grateful love. In gratitude we should bring to

Christ the best we have. The fragrant ointment was a beautiful symbol of a gentle, grateful heart. We, too, should bring to Christ our deepest gratitude and purest affection. No words could express the love Mary bore to her Master, so she put it into an act.

The record says that the house was filled with the odor of the ointment. Indeed, the whole world has been filled since that day with the fragrance of Mary's deed of love and gratitude. It brings joy to the Lord and inspiration to others when his followers do likewise.

The world owes Mary Magdalene a great debt of gratitude in that she was the first to discover the risen Lord. Why was she the first at the tomb of our Saviour? Mary is referred to in Luke's Gospel (8:2) as having been delivered of seven demons. The nature of her infirmities, whether mental or physical, is not entirely clear. Without question her need was very great and her ability to take her place in the world's work and in the Master's new kingdom was sadly limited. Jesus removed her disability, freed her from physical bondage, accepted her ministry, and made her one of his most important messengers of truth.

As Jesus traveled throughout Galilee, "certain women, which had been healed of evil spirits and infirmities" were with him and his disciples. Mary and her associates overlooked the restraints on womanhood in that Eastern land, ignored custom and many comforts that they might show their gratitude to the one who helped them. They wanted to aid him in his task of giving similar help to others. Their desire that their benefactor should benefit others in need gave them courage and a spirit of sacrifice easily underestimated.

Mary's devotion to Jesus led her beyond the discomfort and misunderstandings and criticisms in Galilee. It took her to Jerusalem and to Calvary. She experienced with Jesus the opposition of his enemies in all their passionate bitterness.

In Luke's second reference to Mary Magdalene, she is at the cross. The disciples had fled. This woman who owed so much and was doing so much to repay—her courage did not fail. It had been won at many personal sacrifices. It was worth the price. She and the other women risked everything and remained with the Lord through the crucifixion. They accompanied his body to the grave. After the sabbath rest they came back to complete the preparation for the permanent burial.

Imagine yourself in her place. How deeply she feels! Nothing left now but memories, but how gratefully and tenderly she will do all that can be done on Sunday morning. It is now the only tangible reminder of her deliverer from the seven demons, of the teacher who spoke words of life, of the benefactor whose sympathetic going about doing good brought priceless blessing to her and to many others. How else could she show her gratitude than to attend his last rites? What a privilege the last ministry to his body!

But death is not the power she supposed. The greatest marvel of history takes place. Her despair is changed to hope. Her fear is changed to courage. Do not lose the significance in what took place in Mary's experience that Easter morning as suggested by her two exclamations, "They have taken away my Lord," and, "I have seen the Lord." It is typical of all those who make the new spiritual discovery, typical of every stepping out into a larger, more useful life. Another dedicated, devoted soul has shown her gratitude in action, a pattern worthy of emulation. Gratitude in daily living as expressed by these two Marys is pleasing to God and inspiring to our own lives. But this great Christian virtue loses much of its power to bless, inspire, or help others if it remains only as an attitude of the heart. It is true it must begin there, and it is a fact that God will know the quality and degree of it, but how can it be known to our earthly friends and bring strength, joy, and happiness to their lives unless it is expressed?

One of the strangest stories of the Pacific War is that of an American flier's never forgetting the natives on a faraway island who saved his life after he had been shot down by the Japanese. In late December, 1964, Jack Paar related briefly the thrilling story of Lt. Fred Hargesheimer of White Bear Lake, Minnesota, and presented him to the listening audience. Here is one of the most gripping illustrations of gratitude in action I have ever heard.

Nestling on the northeastern coast of the island of New Britain lies the little village of Nantambu. It is the home of thirty or forty primitive natives of the East Nakani tribe. In World War II, Nantambu was an important barge-staging point for the invading Japanese forces.

In late June, 1943, a lone American flier's plane was shot down by the Japanese over the jagged coastline. Bailing out, he drifted through a tall eucalyptus tree into jungle mud. Except for a gash on his forehead, he was unhurt; but New Britain was heavily occupied by the Japanese, and one hundred miles of wilderness lay between him and his home base in New Guinea.

With only a compass to guide him, he set out through the dense jungle. His emergency rations soon ran out and he became dizzy and weak. After thirty-one days of hunger, loneliness, and despair, he was surprised on the bank of a stream by a group of natives in a canoe. The leader, a dark, wiry fellow, produced a muddy note signed by an Australian officer. It said the old chief, named Lauo, was loyal to the Allies. Overcome with joy, tears trickled down Hargesheimer's face. They gave him some of their meager food and paddled him downstream to their little village.

For five months, as day followed day, with constant threat of being found by the Japanese, he fell desperately ill with malaria. Too weak to eat, a native mother saved his life by feeding him cupfuls of her own milk. Gradually he was well enough to take a few steps. And then one night a strange native arrived with news that the Australians were back in the hills with a wireless. They had been landed on the island to spy on the Japanese.

Guided by the natives he reached their camp. His home base was notified of his safety. A few days later, with two Australian fliers and a group of natives, they made their way to the seacoast where they were picked up by a submarine. They were on their way home.

The war over, Hargesheimer returned to his home in Ohio and married a lovely girl. They have two sons and a daughter. Settling down in a suburb of St. Paul, Minnesota, and leading a pleasant and happy life, he found himself still remembering the New Britain natives who had sheltered him at the risk of their own lives. Why had they done this? They had come under the influence of a lone Christian missionary and were practicing the Samaritanship as taught by our Saviour. In his heart our hero was longing to do something for these primitive people.

After months of prayer and earnest soul searching, the family agreed to forego their vacation, and with money borrowed from his bank, he set out on his sentimental journey in 1960. Uppermost in his mind was the question, Would they remember the American flier they had rescued seventeen years previously? As the old rusty trawler neared the little coastal village, he could see a group of natives on the beach. Among them was Lauo, the old chief with whom he had had his first contact. Recognition was immediate, and great was the rejoicing and celebration. His visit was brief, but a vision of some definite help for his beloved friends was his reward.

Back in St. Paul he met with Protestant missionaries. They gave him advice and encouragement. After his contacting many of his fellow airmen, the Airmen's Nantambu Memorial Foundation was established. After two-and-one-half years' work they had been able to raise $15,000 for building three units of a school, 10,000 miles away in a tropical jungle. Education was one of the natives' greatest needs.

In June, 1963, Hargesheimer and his husky seventeen-year-old son set out again for New Britain. With the generous help of an Australian contractor and willing natives, this man with a grateful heart saw the beginnings of his dream come true. After six weeks the work was almost finished. In February, 1964, the three buildings, containing four classrooms and an assembly hall, opened. A school was started, staffed by one Australian teacher, two native teachers, and administered by the Australian government. One hundred and thirty children came by foot and dugout canoes from surrounding villages to be ministered to. Why? Because one man was determined to demonstrate his gratitude to these humble, uneducated people who had learned the meaning of God's love for them and for all men.

"Oh that men would praise the Lord for his goodness, and for his wonderful works to the children of men!" (Psalm 107:8). As we revel in the bounties from his hand, may we be grateful for the love that hath redeemed us, for the providence that shelters us, for the discipline that at times chastens us, and the patience that he bears with us. It is for him, not his manifold gifts, that we should be grateful.

16
Today, and Our Tomorrows

"To awaken each morning with a smile brightening my face; to greet the day with reverence for the opportunities it contains; to approach my work with a clean mind; to hold ever before me, even in the doing of little things, the Ultimate Purpose toward which I am working, to meet men and women with laughter on my lips and love in my heart; to be gentle, kind and courteous through all the hours; to approach the night with weariness that ever woos sleep and with the joy that comes from work well done—this is how I desire to waste wisely my days." [1]

"This is the day which the Lord hath made; we will rejoice and be glad in it" (Psalm 118:24).

What beautiful patterns for every day, first from a dedicated Christian, and then from the psalmist.

Daniel Webster, brilliant American statesman and a member of President Fillmore's Cabinet, many years ago gave us a new appraisal and appreciation of how much just one day should mean to every grateful heart.

---

[1] *Today Is Mine,* comp. and ed. Thomas Curtis Clark (New York: Harper & Row, 1950), p. 138. Used by permission.

The morning itself, few inhabitants of cities know anything about. Among all our good people, not one in a thousand sees the sun rise once a year. They know nothing of the morning. Their idea of it is that it is that part of the day which comes along after a cup of coffee and a piece of toast. With them, morning is not a new issuing of light, a new bursting forth of the sun, a new waking-up of all that has life from a sort of temporary death, to behold again the works of God, the heavens and the earth; it is only a part of the domestic day, belonging to reading papers, answering notes, sending the children to school, and giving orders for dinner.

The first streak of light, the earliest purpling of the east, which the lark springs up to greet, and the deeper and deeper coloring, into orange and red, till at length the "glorious sun is seen, regent of the day"—this they never enjoy, for they never see it.

I never thought that Adam had much the advantage of us from having seen the world while it was new. The manifestations of the power of God, like his mercies, are new every morning and fresh every moment. We see as fine rising of the sun as ever Adam saw; and its risings are as much a miracle now as they were in his day—and, I think, a good deal more, because it is now a part of the miracle, that for thousands and thousands of years He has come to His appointed time, without the variation of a millionth part of a second.

I know the morning, I am acquainted with it, and I love it. I love it fresh and sweet as it is—a daily new creation, breaking forth and calling all that have life and breath and being to a new adoration, new enjoyments, and new gratitude.

Note "The Salutation of the Dawn," based on the Sanskrit, written about 1200 B.C.:

> Listen to the Exhortation of the Dawn!
> Look to this Day!
> For it is Life, the very Life of Life.

In its brief course lie all
Verities and Realities of your Existence:
   The Bliss of Growth,
   The Glory of Action,
   The splendor of Beauty,
For yesterday is but a Dream,
And To-morrow is only a Vision:
But To-day well lived makes
   Every Yesterday a Dream of Happiness,
   And every To-morrow a Vision of Hope.
   Look well therefore to this Day!
   Such is the Salutation of the Dawn.

We ought to make the most and best of the present, with
its opportunities, just where our lot is cast. If the past has
been dark, we have the better chance to make up for it. If it
has been brighter than our present lot, we do not make
things better by needless comparisons which only emphasize
the gloom that may have enshrouded our lives. And if the
future, perchance, holds in store for us some grief or suffering or loss, we shall be the better able to endure it, for joy
gives strength. "Be not therefore anxious for the morrow: for
the morrow will be anxious for itself. Sufficient unto the day
is the evil thereof" (Matt. 6:34, ASV).

Several years ago, Kenneth L. Holmes, then dean of men
at Linfield College, McMinnville, Oregon, had occasion to
try and help two of his friends make contact with Alcoholics
Anonymous. From them Dr. Holmes received a little folder
entitled "Just for Today" in which a pattern for living was
outlined for these unfortunate men. It has a message for
everyone—a challenging message.

Just for today I will try to live through this day only, and not
tackle my whole life problem at once. I can do something for

twelve hours that would appall me if I felt that I had to keep it up for a lifetime.

Just for today, I will be happy. This assumes . . . that "most folks are as happy as they make up their minds to be". . . .

Just for today I will try to strengthen my mind. I will study. I will learn something useful. I will not be a mental loafer. I will read something that requires effort, thought and concentration.

Just for today, I will adjust myself to what is, and not try everything to my own desires. I will take my "luck" as it comes, and fit myself to it.

Just for today, I will exercise my soul in three ways: I will do somebody a good turn, and not get found out. I will do at least two things I don't want to do—just for exercise. I will not show anyone that my feelings are hurt; they may be hurt, but today I will not show it.

Just for today, I will be agreeable. I will look as well as I can, dress becomingly, talk low, act courteously, criticize not one bit, not find fault with anything and not try to improve or regulate anybody except myself.

Just for today, I will have a program. I may not follow it exactly, but I will have it. I will save myself from two pests: hurry and indecision.

Just for today, I will *have a quiet half hour all by myself,* and relax. During this half hour, sometime, I will try to get a better perspective of my life.

Just for today, I will *be unafraid.* Especially I will not be afraid to enjoy what is beautiful, and to believe that as I give to the world, so the world will give to me.

To lift ourselves from the level of living as practiced by so much of the world, how blessed, how rewarded we would be if some time every day we would just take a few minutes and turn our thoughts Godward. There are so many areas of life in which God can help us, and in which we can be a blessing, if we will think about him at opportune times.

"My voice shalt thou hear in the morning, O Lord; in the morning will I direct my prayer unto thee, and will look up."

Walter Russell Bowie, in his devotional manual of prayers and meditations entitled *Lift Up Your Hearts,* gives us a heart-warming pattern for the day, "A Meditation on the Lord's Prayer."

Our Father, who art in heaven.
Help me to believe this day that there is a power to lift me up which is stronger than all the things that hold me down.
Hallowed be Thy Name.
Help me to be sensitive to what is beautiful, and responsive to what is good, so that day by day I may grow more sure of the holiness of life in which I want to trust.
Thy Kingdom come.
Help me to be quick to see, and ready to encourage, whatever brings the better meaning of God into that which otherwise might be the common round of the uninspired day.
Thy will be done on earth, as it is in heaven.
Help me to believe that the ideals of the spirit are not a far-off dream, but a power to command loyalty and direct my life here on our real earth.
Give us this day our daily bread.
Open the way for me to earn an honest living without anxiety; but let me never forget the needs of others, and make me want only that benefit for myself which will also be their gain.
And forgive us our trespasses, as we forgive those who trespass against us.
Make me patient and sympathetic with the shortcomings of others, especially of those I love; and keep me sternly watchful only of my own. Let me never grow hard with the unconscious cruelty of those who measure themselves by mean standards, and so think they have excelled. Keep my eyes lifted to the highest, so that I may be forgiving, because I know how much there is of which I need to be forgiven.

And lead us not into temptation, but deliver us from evil.
Let me not go carelessly this day within the reach of any evil I
cannot resist, but if in the path of duty I must go where temptation is, give me strength of spirit to meet it without fear.
*For thine is the kingdom, and the power, and the glory for ever
and ever. Amen.*[2]

"Day by day we magnify Thee," in our prayers, in our
witnessing, in our gratitude, in our service to others. On the
place mats of a restaurant in Gatlinburg, Tennessee, there
are brief prayers for several faiths, and the Protestant prayer
reads, "Bless, O Lord, this food to our use and us to Thy
service, and make us ever mindful of the *needs of others*, in
Jesus' name. Amen." Having set your motives and embraced
the broad principles of righteousness, it does not do to look
too far ahead. With the proper background each day should
be complete in itself, our very best having been poured into
it. It isn't the experience of today that at times drives men
mad. It is the remorse of what happened yesterday and the
fear of what tomorrow might bring. These are God's days
. . . today and tomorrow . . . leave them to him.

A son was called home because his mother was very seriously
ill. She lived in a little cottage on the shore of the great Pacific
Ocean. Throughout their lives there had been a warm bond of
love and understanding which had held them closely together. It
was not easy for the boy now to see his mother at the end of the
journey and to think of the loneliness which would be his until
some day they would meet again.

The day was far spent and the evening shadows were beginning to fall. The sun was setting in majestic glory over the great
body of water which only God would have the power to create.

---

[2] (Nashville: Abingdon Press, 1956), pp. 13–15. Used by permission.

It streamed through the window and reflected in the radiant face of this saint of God who was on her way home. The boy got up to pull down the shade whereupon the mother turned to him and feebly whispered, "Ernest, don't pull down the shade." They both silently looked for a moment into the faraway horizon. The great Artist had splashed the colors of gold and amber and red upon the tapestry of the evening sky and, evidently thinking of the old adage, "Red sunset at night, sailors' delight," this Christian woman of great faith turned to her boy and said, "Ernest, tomorrow is going to be a glorious day!"

Her words were most prophetic. By the time morning came her soul had been carried by angel wings into the eternal paradise of God. She had claimed the promises of Christ her Saviour and now she knew the reality of all that she had ever hoped for.

When we have faith to believe we, too, live in the promise of tomorrow being more glorious than today. Life can be lived on the ascendancy. Every step goes higher, higher. Each day is more glorious than the one that has preceded it. And life's final day is the most glorious of all for it means the life of God without earthly separations and sorrow and sin.[3]

Today is mine! Recall the mistakes you may have made today. Resolve to correct them that tomorrow may find you reaching higher. "This is the day which the Lord hath made: we will rejoice and be glad in it" (Psalm 118:24).

---

[3] Reuben K. Youngdahl, *Going God's Way* (Rock Island, Ill.: Augustana Book Concern, 1951), p. 7.

Other Broadman Books by
R. L. Middleton

The Accents of Life

Don't Disappoint God

God So Loved, He Gave

The Goodness of God

My Cup Runneth Over

Thinking About God

Youth Conquering for Christ

Youth's Talents for Christ

Date Due

BROADMAN
B | **P**
SUPPLIES

Code 4386-04, CLS-4, Broadman Supplies, Nashville, Tenn.,
Printed in U.S.A.